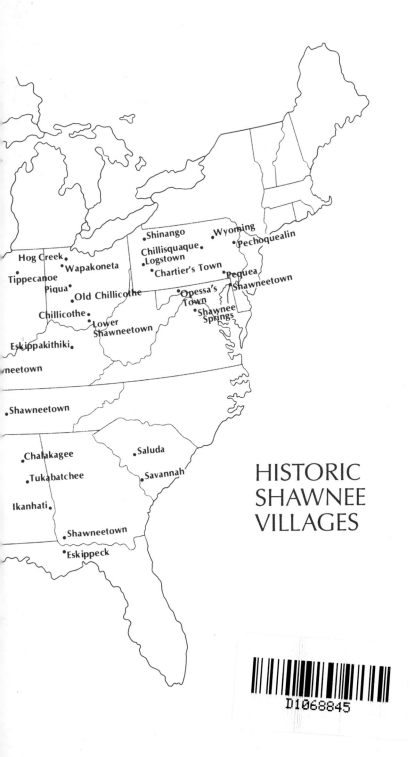

HISTORIC
SHAWNEE
VILLAGES

Shinango
Wyoming
Pechoquealin
Chillisquaque
Hog Creek
Logstown
Wapakoneta
Chartier's Town
Pequea
Tippecanoe
Shawneetown
Piqua
Opessa's
Old Chillicothe
Town
Chillicothe
Shawnee
Lower
Springs
Shawneetown
Eskippakithiki
neetown

Shawneetown

Chalakagee
Saluda
Tukabatchee
Savannah
Ikanhati

Shawneetown
Eskippeck

D1068845

The
Shawnee

The Shawnee

JERRY E. CLARK

THE UNIVERSITY PRESS OF KENTUCKY

Copyright © 1993 by The University Press of Kentucky

Scholarly publisher for the Commonwealth,
serving Bellarmine College, Berea College, Centre
College of Kentucky, Eastern Kentucky University,
The Filson Club, Georgetown College, Kentucky
Historical Society, Kentucky State University,
Morehead State University, Murray State University,
Northern Kentucky University, Transylvania University,
University of Kentucky, University of Louisville,
and Western Kentucky University.

Editorial and Sales Offices: Lexington, Kentucky 40508-4008

Library of Congress Cataloging-in-Publication Data

Clark, Jerry E.
  The Shawnee / Jerry E. Clark.
    p.   cm.
  Includes bibliographical references and index.
  ISBN 0-8131-1839-5 (alk. paper) :
  1. Shawnee Indians—History.   2. Shawnee Indians—Social life and
customs.   I. Title.
E99.S35C56   1993
973′.04973—dc20   93-14114

To my son, Anthony

Contents

Acknowledgments

I would like to acknowledge the help of those who have contributed their time and effort to this book: the archivists, librarians, and colleagues who located sources and offered helpful comments, criticisms, and support; Anthony Colson, Mary Wilma Hargreaves, Margaret Lantis, and the late Philip Drucker, who made useful suggestions; and Frances Mitchell and Judy Bauer, who aided in the final preparation of the manuscript. A special thanks must go to Lathel Duffield, who generated my interest in the Shawnee and who was my constant critic and support throughout the entire project. Finally, I would like to thank Martha Ellen Webb, who spent countless hours preparing the index for this work.

1

INTRODUCTION

Most of the accepted histories indicate that there were no permanent Indian settlements in Kentucky during historic times. Yet stories abound of the presence of Indians, particularly Shawnee, in many regions of Kentucky. Stories of whites held in Indian captivity and of Indians working in Swift's silver mines come from the mountains of eastern Kentucky. From the central part of the state come tales of Indian attacks on the new, and fortified, settlements of Harrodsburg and Boonesboro.

How can these inconsistencies be reconciled? Could it be that the Shawnee only ventured into Kentucky to intimidate the white settlers and then retreated to their settlements north of the Ohio River, as historians have noted? Certainly there are few documented Indian villages in Kentucky during historic times. Eskippakithiki, the Shawnee settlement in Clark County, was abandoned in 1754. This was the most famous of the Kentucky Indian settlements and, except for a small settlement near Limestone, Kentucky, across from the Scioto River, the only one whose exact location is known.

The question arises, then, why the Shawnee would bother to raid white settlements if there was no threat to their villages. Another question, equally perplexing, is why a state so rich in prehistoric village sites would have been avoided by historic Indians. Kentucky was settled relatively late in colonial times, and there would have been few pressures to drive the Indians from the area.

One reason for the apparent inconsistencies may lie in the lack of understanding of the Shawnee people by the whites in the early period. The Shawnee were nomadic at least part of the year, when they moved their small family settlements in pursuit of game. They considered the land free to be used by any Indian group who had need of it. In the summer they settled in rather large villages where they raised crops of corn, beans, and squash. Smaller family bands moved regularly in the winter and established rather impermanent settlements as they hunted deer, bison, and other meat- and hide-producing animals. Though Kentucky was a favored hunting area for the Shawnee, the lack of permanent year-round villages may have given the false impression that the region was not occupied by Shawnee.

After American independence, most of the identified summer villages were located north of the Ohio River. But the Shawnee also considered Kentucky as their own. In 1769 a group of Shawnee had warned Daniel Boone to leave Kentucky, because it belonged to them. When he did not obey, it cost Boone the life of a son. So Kentucky was occupied, perhaps not in the sense of being secured by European-style settlements and towns, but frequented by a group of Indians who used it and called it their own.

The lack of records of Indian settlements in Kentucky may also have been partly by the design of land speculators. Even before the Revolution, speculators had cast a covetous eye on the fertile and beautiful land in Kentucky. Several schemes launched by colonial traders, and even by Benjamin Franklin, to acquire large tracts of land south of the Ohio had gone awry. With the end of the French and Indian War, the Virginia colonial government gave large bonuses to soldiers in the form of military tracts. Surveyors were sent to Kentucky to lay out plots for various clients, including George Washington. Daniel Boone spent a great deal of his time laying out tracts of his own for future settlement. (Once while on a mission to warn a

2

village of a pending Indian attack, he delayed long enough to mark out and survey a piece of land.)

To realize a profit from the sale of this land, speculators had to attract settlers who would purchase land and establish communities. If potential settlers knew they would face possible threats from Indians, they might remain in the East rather than migrate west. Speculators needed buyers as well as a large number of able-bodied men to develop and pacify the area. Once a man invested all he had to move to Kentucky, it was not likely that he would return. Thus the failure to mention the presence of Indians may have been a ploy to gain settlers. The literature used to attract such settlers emphasized the fertile soil and rich supplies of game, but never mentioned the Shawnee. Certainly explorers and speculators such as Daniel Boone, Thomas Bullitt, and James Harrod knew of the Indians. And the settlers soon learned of and felt the presence of the Shawnee. Favored hunting territory would not be given up easily, and the Shawnee resistance to white settlement was fierce.

The Shawnee were and are Algonquian speakers. They probably numbered between 2,000 and 4,000 individuals during the early historic period. In 1825 a census of Indian tribes in the United States enumerated a total of 2,293 Shawnee. By that date wars and European diseases may have reduced the Shawnee population. The census figure, however, does not include the Shawnee who were residing in Texas at the time.

The name Shawnee comes from the Algonquian term "Shawan" meaning "south" or "Shawunogi" meaning "southerner." The French called the Shawnee "Chaouanons." The Iroquois, with whom the Shawnee historically maintained a hostile relationship, called them "Ontwaganha," meaning "those who utter unintelligible speech." In fact there are some 150 different names and spellings that have been used to refer to the Shawnee.

Until they were removed west of the Missouri River in 1832, migration was a way of life for the Shawnee. The wide-

3

spread distribution of Shawnee names for historical and contemporary towns, rivers, and other places gives evidence of the highly mobile nature of these people. This movement has perplexed historians and made it difficult to get a clear picture of the tribe. One difficulty is in trying to determine a home territory for them. However, if one looks at the earliest historic locations and at traditional claims by the Shawnee, it appears that at least a tentative case can be made for the Ohio and Cumberland valleys. This places the present state of Kentucky at the center of the Shawnee homeland.

2

HISTORY OF
THE SHAWNEE

LINGUISTICALLY THE Shawnee are identifiable with the group of Central Algonquian speakers including the Miami, Kickapoo, Illiniwek, and Sauk and Fox, among others. In early historic times, as their name implies, they were the southernmost of this group. The original home of the entire Algonquian stock lay somewhere in the eastern subarctic region of Canada. The hunting and fishing practices of the Algonquian-speaking groups have led scholars to believe that the early Algonquians probably lived in the vicinity of Lake Winnipeg. It is thought that the Shawnee were one of the earliest groups to move south from this area. However, the precise route taken, the length of time spent in the migration, and even the approximate time of departure are unknown. Thus it is difficult to separate fact from fiction when dealing with tribal legend and tradition.

The Walam Olum, the migration legend of the Delaware, gives a clue about the time of the Shawnee migration to the south: "When Little Fog was chief, many of them [Delaware] went away with the Nanticoke and Shawnee to the land in the south." The date of this occurrence is estimated at about 1240 A.D. Later, the tradition states, "when White Horn was chief, they were in the region of the Talega Mountains and there also were the Illinois, the Shawnee, and the Conoy." The very next verse mentions a landlocked lake, suggesting that the region occupied was the area from the Alleghenies or upper Ohio River to Lake Erie. The estimated time for this occupation is about 1500.

Some Central Algonquians, particularly the Sauk and Fox, have preserved a tradition of migrating from the Atlantic down the Saint Lawrence to the Great Lakes. So perhaps they moved east first and then came back west and south. The Sauk and Fox also maintain, and linguistic evidence supports this, that the Shawnee belong to the same stock as themselves.

The Kickapoo, located in the Great Lakes region, and the Shawnee also were related, and the two tribes share a legend about their separation. The split, it is said, was caused by a hunters' quarrel over the division of some roasted bear paws. The only difference as the tale is told by the two tribes is that each lays the blame for the incident on the other. Major Morrell Marston, a commander of a frontier post in the 1820s, tells of a Shawnee chief who describes the same incident, except that it was the Sauk and not the Kickapoo from which the Shawnee separated.

This early location in the Great Lakes region is supported by the anthropologist Erminie W. Voegelin. Basing her analysis largely upon burial practices, she concludes that before the arrival of the Europeans the various Shawnee divisions were located in the northeastern part of the Great Lakes region, for their strongest cultural affiliations are with the Huron, Seneca, Winnebago, Ojibwa, Delaware, and Nanticoke. From here the Shawnee apparently continued in a southwesterly direction, for the Ohio Valley yields the strongest archaeological evidence of late prehistoric Shawnee occupation.

In the Ohio Valley, the Fort Ancient is the latest prehistoric archaeological culture. Named for the Fort Ancient earthworks in Warren County, Ohio (later discovered to belong to an earlier archaeological culture), the Fort Ancient people were related to the Mississippian peoples who constructed the large mounds at Cahokia, near Saint Louis, Missouri. The Fort Ancient people, however, lived in smaller villages and raised corn in the river bottoms of southern Ohio and Indiana and in northern Kentucky. Although they often buried their dead in small mounds within the village, the Fort Ancient people did not construct large temple mounds such as those found in the Mississippian culture to the west. Just as the Mississippian culture had mysteriously disappeared by the time Europeans set foot in the area, so too the Fort Ancient culture was gone. It may be that the people who had developed and carried on the prehistoric culture were forced to abandon the area. But more likely they had obtained such a large inventory of European trade goods from other Indians in more direct contact with whites that their material culture no longer resembled what was left behind at Fort Ancient sites. Thus the tribal affiliation of the Fort Ancient culture is difficult to identify.

Historians have not agreed upon the ethnic identity of Fort Ancient peoples, and more evidence is needed before any conclusive statement can be made. But what evidence there is seems to point in part to Algonquian speakers. Madisonville, one of the largest Fort Ancient sites, located on the Little Miami River near its mouth on the Ohio River approximately at the site of the present city of Cincinnati, contained European trade goods. It has been identified both as a Shawnee and and as a Mosopelea village. However, the Mosopelea identification is based on a 1684 map by Franquelin, who at La Salle's request showed eight Mosopelean villages located in this region, while Marquette and Joliet had found the Mosopelea well below the Ohio River on the Mississippi. Archaeologist James B. Griffin believes that the Madisonville site is probably Shawnee. Erminie Voegelin disagrees and places the center of the Shawnee well to the east, in New York and eastern Pennsylvania, but most other anthropologists feel that the weight of linguistic, ethnohistorical, archaeological, and physical evidence indicates that the Shawnee were indeed the descendants of the Fort Ancient populations.

An archaeological site near Starved Rock on the Illinois River was occupied in historical times by a group of Shawnee, who with other Indians, joined La Salle after he constructed Fort Saint Louis at this location in 1682. This site contained material very similar to Fort Ancient material, and may be attributable to the Shawnee, though some anthropologists have identified the Fort Ancient-like material as Miami or Illinois.

The Fort Ancient culture is not the only prehistoric complex to have been identified with the Shawnee. Cyrus Thomas attributes a Shawnee ethnicity to the smaller stone box burial mounds at the Etowah site in Georgia. However, since stone box graves were used over several centuries by a variety of cultural groups, these could have been constructed by any one of several tribes in the East.

One reason it is difficult to identify the Shawnee in archaeological sites is that the criteria used to define an archaeological culture are in large measure distinguished on the basis of the material artifacts and structural remains. In any area, artifacts and other cultural material are freely borrowed and adapted by a variety of ethnic groups, making it difficult to distinguish these groups on material traits alone. A great deal of disruption and change of the native population had already taken place in the Ohio Valley before any direct observations of tribal locations were recorded. Therefore it cannot be assumed that local prehistoric remains belong to the ethnic group first recorded in that area.

Early historic references to the Shawnee also raise problems of identification. Since the term "Shawnee" means southerner, it may have been applied to many Algonquian and non-Algonquian speakers existing south of the main body. Another problem concerns the history of the various Shawnee divisions. The Shawnee are comprised of five named divisions: Chillicothe, Hathawekela, Kispogogi, Mequachake, and Piqua. The question is whether the Shawnee represent an amalgamation of originally distinct tribes or a single group that later subdivided. This question becomes important in interpreting the early history of the Shawnee. If the Shawnee represent disparate tribes that confederated, then it is necessary to find them located together in the late prehistoric or early historic period for a sufficient time to develop a common language and a common culture. If, on the other hand, these divisions represent a single tribe which split into semiautonomous groups, then one would not be surprised to find them dwelling in widely separated locations even in the early historic times.

There are basically two interpretations regarding the early historic locations of the Shawnee. The first views the Shawnee as situated in the Northeast as a single tribe until the Iroquois confederacy forced them down the Ohio River and drove them to the southern branches of the Ohio by the second half of the seventeenth century. From here they split into rather autonomous divisions. The second interpretation has them drifting southward prior to European settlement along the eastern piedmont through Virginia, the Carolinas, and Georgia. From Georgia some Shawnee groups went west toward the Mississippi River. Towards the end of the seventeenth century they began moving back to the north, uniting finally in the Ohio Valley as a single group.

There is little in the historic record to support the premise of an extensive Shawnee occupation in the Southeast at such an early date. One possible bit of evidence for the theory is the village of Chalaque on the Savannah River near present-day Augusta, Georgia. In 1540 De Soto's party visited this community where he found a group of hunters and gatherers. Most historians have identified these people as Cherokee, but the Muskogee term "Chilokee" means "the people of a different speech" and may have been applied to non-Cherokee people as well. Chalaque might also suggest a form of Chillicothe, a division of the Shawnee, and supports the tradition of a southeastern origin for this division.

In 1584 Ralph Dane, commander-in-chief of Sir Walter Raleigh's colony at Roanoke, made reference to a town of about 700 fighting men, 130 miles from Roanoke, called Chawanock. This town also appears on John White's map of 1586. Captain John Smith, who arrived in the New World in 1607, referred to the Chawanocks as living in Virginia, where they continued in dwindling numbers for some time. That the Chawanocks were Shawnee is questionable, but the North Carolina location is only 400 miles from De Soto's Chalaque. "Chawanock" is very similar to "Sawanwake," a plural name for Shawnee, and also brings to mind the Shawnee tradition that there were originally six divisions, the most powerful of which, the Shawano, became extinct.

Indications of Shawnee locations in the Northeast are more numerous. In 1603 the Satanas or Shawanoes lived on the banks of the lakes in western New York, south of Lake Erie. When Captain John Smith first arrived in Virginia, the Iroquois were fighting a fierce war against the allied Mohicans, residing on Long Island, and Shawanoes on the Susquehanna River. Dutch and Swedish navigator maps as early as 1614 place a nation called the "Sawwanew" on the east bank of the Delaware River (but the Delaware River was at that date known as "South" River and Sawwanew may have been a general term applied to any Indians residing on that river). Also in 1632, Captain Henry Fleet mentioned a town called "Shaunetowa" at the head of navigation of the Potomac. The Moravian missionary John Heckewelder associated the Pequots, who were involved in a bloody war with the Massachusetts colonists in 1637, with the Piqua division of the Shawnee. Vandernock's map of 1656 locates a village of "Sauwanoos" between the upper Schuylkill and the Delaware, and on a 1676 map of New Netherlands by Roggeveen the "Sauno" had a village near the mouth of the Schuylkill.

Even if all these references apply to the Shawnee, they account for only a small portion of the tribe. Apparently most of the Shawnee occupied the country farther west, beyond white contacts and the reach of historical observation. Though direct evidence is lacking, there is indirect evidence that at least a portion of the Shawnee occupied the Ohio Valley during this early historic period. In June 1732, the Shawnee sent a letter to Governor Gordon of Pennsylvania in which they stated that about five years before, the Five Nations of the Iroquois had ordered the Shawnee to return to Ohio, where they had come from. This can be interpreted to mean that around 1670 the Shawnee had lived on the Cumberland River and on the Ohio between the mouths of the Muskingum and the Wabash. As a further indication of the early Ohio connection, in 1758 when Chief Paxinosa was asked where he and his family were going when they left Pennsylvania, he replied: "To my land at the Ohio, where I was born."

There are numerous references to the wars of the Iroquois which indicate that in the mid-seventeenth century they drove the Shawnee from the area south of Lake Erie. But the Iroquois did not confine their war to the region immediately south of the lake. In 1666 a group of Seneca captured some Shawnee near the Mississippi River probably south of the Ohio. If the Iroquois extended their hostilities for such great distances it is quite possible that their encounters with the Shawnee could have been in the Cumberland region or the lower Ohio Valley.

The Ohio Valley may have been the center for the main body of Shawnee into the early seventeenth century. But by mid-century it is apparent that they were spread over a wide area from present-day Ohio to the Cumberland River and quite possibly even as far west as the Mississippi River. As early as 1648 there were Shawnee residing with the Mascoutins in Illinois. The *Jesuit Relations* of 1661–1662 tell of Shawnee located some 1,000 miles west of the Iroquois along a beautiful river, probably the Ohio. The Seneca warned La Salle in 1669 of the ferocity of the Shawnee, and Galinée, La Salle's chronicler, said that the Shawnee lived about a month's journey from the source of the Ohio River. One of the latest accounts that may refer to the Shawnee on the Ohio River in the seventeenth century comes from Gabriel Arthur, who as a captive of the Cherokee in 1674 traveled some three days from the Great Kanawha River to strike a blow against a powerful nation to the west, believed to have been the Shawnee. This may have been a group pushing north and east from the Cumberland region.

By 1680 the principal locations of the Shawnee were in the Cumberland Valley and along the Savannah River in South Carolina. They had migrated either to the mouth of the Ohio and up the Cumberland and Tennessee rivers or over the Great Warriors Path southward across Kentucky. Some had gone north into the territories of the Miami and Illinois Indians in the vicinity of Lake Michigan. In 1684 the Iroquois justified an attack on the Miami on the grounds that the latter had invited the Shawnee into the country for the purpose of making war on the Iroquois. In 1682 La Salle completed Fort Saint Louis on the Illinois River at Starved Rock; and the Illiniwek, who had earlier abandoned this location because of Iroquois raids, returned. The Shawnee, including one group called by that name and others called by La Salle the Chaskepe, Ouabano, and Cisca (names of the various Shawnee villages or bands), also settled the area near the fort. This involved a considerable movement to the Illinois River from the lower Cumberland region in Tennessee and Kentucky. But less than ten years later this large group had moved eastward to Maryland and Pennsylvania.

Historian John R. Swanton suggests that the Shawnee may have been attracted to the Cumberland region partly by the Spanish post in Saint Augustine, Florida, which they visited in order to trade. This explanation would certainly account for the settlement in the Savannah River valley of South Carolina. Shawnee knowledge of and expeditions to the Spanish trading posts may have come quite early. In 1662 Father Lalement, a French Jesuit, indicated that the Shawnee were already trading with the Spanish in Florida. Marquette also mentioned Shawnee-Spanish trade in 1673, and Spanish trade beads were found among the Shawnee of South Carolina in 1674. At La Salle's request the Shawnee who settled near Fort Saint Louis agreed to abandon the Spanish trade.

Most of the maps dating from 1670 call what is today the Cumberland River the "Rivière des Chaouanons." In fact it was identified as the Shawnee River until nearly the end of the eighteenth century. When the early French traders came into this area in the 1670s, the Shawnee had a principal village on the Cumberland River, near the present site of Nashville, which had been occupied as early as 1665.

It is difficult to know the precise locations of the various Shawnee villages because of the inaccuracies or incompleteness of many of these early maps. Three maps were published in 1674, all of which place the "Chaouanons" near the mouth of the Ohio River. Marquette locates several Shawnee villages east of the mouth of the Ohio, but does not extend the Ohio far enough east so that the relationship of these villages to the river can be determined. Both Randin and Joliet place the Shawnee south of the Ohio River, the former on the Mississippi and the latter in the vicinity of a tributary, probably the Cumberland, which flows north to the Ohio near its mouth. Based on the accounts of La Salle, the maps of Franquelin in 1684 and 1688 contain much more detail. The information on the Kentucky-Tennessee area undoubtedly came from the Shawnee who had settled at Starved Rock by 1683. On the map of 1684 the main river emptying into the Mississippi from the east is the Casquinampogama (Tennessee), and it has several tributaries including the Wabash and Ohio rivers. The westernmost river to flow into the Tennessee is the Misseoucipi (not to be confused with the Mississippi) and the next is labeled "Skipaki-cipi, ou la Rivière Bleue." Between these rivers is the Shawnee village of Cisca, with a path leading to Saint Petro on the coast of Florida and a legend that translates: "Path by which the Shawnee trade with the Spanish." In 1683 the inhabitants of Cisca and other Shawnee joined the French at Fort Saint Louis on the Illinois River. On this same map the village of "Meguatchaiki" is situated on the north bank of the Skipakicipi River, probably a village of the Mequachake division. The Skipakicipi River is undoubtedly the Green, named, perhaps, after the Kispogogi division, but the identity of the Misseoucipi is not clear. It is probably the Red or the Licking River.

The name "Taogria" appears on at least one map as a village on the Cumberland River quite near seven Shawnee villages. In 1699 Gravier, a Jesuit explorer, encountered a party of Taogria on the Mississippi River above Memphis, Tennessee, and identified them as belonging to the Loup Nation. Swanton believes they were Yuchi. However, they spoke the Chaouanon tongue and may have been Shawnee. Other maps of the period locate Taogria villages along the Ohio and Tennessee rivers, usually near Shawnee villages. Galinée, La

Salle's chronicler, may have provided a clue to the identity of the Taogria when he reported that in 1669 the Seneca warned him of a bad and treacherous people on the Ohio called the Toagenha. The Iroquois referred to the Shawnee as the Ontwaganha, and it is probable that Toagenha is a corruption of this term. The similarity of the names Toagenha and Taogria suggests a possible link.

From their location on the Cumberland in the late seventeenth century various Shawnee bands traveled widely, visiting and even settling in scattered areas from Illinois to Florida. Trade with the Spanish in Florida has already been mentioned, and certain Shawnee traditions indicate that a village or villages may have been established there. In 1707 a southern Indian taken captive to Virginia drew a map on which he placed a village called Ephippeck (Eskippeck) on the Apalachicola River, in the panhandle of Florida. This could be a Shawnee settlement from the group identified with the Skipakicipi River in Kentucky, and possibly the group that later returned to build Eskippakithiki in Clark County, Kentucky. This tends to support an account of the Shawnee Black Hoof that in his childhood he lived near the sea in Florida.

There are also indications that the Shawnee had a village near the Creek Indians in Alabama before 1685. In addition the "Salt" Indians situated on the Kanawha River a little above present-day Charleston, West Virginia, as described by Fallows in 1671, are believed to have been Shawnee. This band may have been migrating south from the Ohio Valley when they established a temporary village and made a supply of salt.

During their stay in the Cumberland region the Shawnee came under the influence of British traders from South Carolina and in 1699, led by these traders, made an attack on a group of Cahokia Indians on the Mississippi River fifteen miles below the mouth of the Illinois River. It was very possibly this British alliance that caused the Cherokee and Chickasaw to expel the Shawnee from the Cumberland in 1714. Another possibility is that the war was a result of Chickasaw efforts to bring the Shawnee more closely under French influence. In any case some of the Shawnee escaped into the Creek country of Alabama, but most began working their way north to the Ohio and eventually to Pennsylvania.

Some of the Shawnee bands may not have moved farther away than what is today the eastern part of Kentucky. Kentucky historian Lucien Beckner suggests that the village of Eskippakithiki, in Clark County, Kentucky, may have been originally settled by a party of those fleeing from the Cumberland River. This may have been the group situated on the Apalachicola River in 1707 who moved north settling first at present-day Nashville and driven from there to Eskippakithiki by 1718.

Eskippakithiki is a Shawnee word meaning "blue lick place." The village was favorably located near present-day Winchester on a hill above Lulbegrud Creek. The site was, as the name implies, near a salt lick, which attracted large numbers of deer. It was also situated along the Great Warriors Path, the major trail leading from villages in Ohio to the Cumberland River and on to the South. Besides Beckner's interpretation, there are many other theories about the origin of this village, but there was apparently no white contact there until 1752. Charles Hanna, in *The Wilderness Trail*, states that he believes it was not established until 1745, when he thinks Peter Chartier stopped there for two years after fleeing from Pennsylvania. But there is good evidence to support an earlier origin. There were some 3,500 acres of land cleared by the Shawnee in the vicinity of Indian Old Fields, as Eskippakithiki is now called. Basing his estimate on the time required to deaden and completely remove by burning the great oaks, hickories, sycamores, gums, and maples from such an area, Willard Jillson, noted Kentucky historian and naturalist, set the founding of the village at 1680 to 1685. Such an early date is possible in that Shawnee groups escaping the Iroquois down the Great Warriors Path would have passed through this area. Another interpretation is that a band from Carolina broke away in 1730 and formed a village on Lulbegrud Creek.

If one is to believe Black Hoof's claim that he was born at Eskippakithiki, then the interpretation of Lucien Beckner or Jillson appears to be closer to the truth.

Eskippakithiki is an interesting and important village for the Shawnee. According to Beckner it was originally built by a group belonging to the Piqua division, and he believes this to be the village listed in the 1736 French census as containing some two hundred men. It is almost certain that Eskippakithiki was the home of one of the most famous of the Shawnee chiefs, Cathecassa, better known as Black Hoof. Several sources mention him in relation to this village and Black Hoof himself claimed to have been born there (though other sources place his birth in Florida). Black Hoof was the chief of the Chillicothe division as well as the recognized chief of the entire Shawnee tribe. Besides being a great orator, he was a fierce war leader and a major target in the wars between Shawnee and whites in Ohio and Kentucky until the Treaty of Greenville in 1795. After the treaty, however, he made peace with the whites, and even Tecumseh was unsuccessful in getting him to join in later hostilities against them. He died at Wapakoneta in 1831 at the supposed age of one hundred and ten years.

In 1752 a Virginia trader named John Finley was invited by the Shawnee to build a house at Eskippakithiki, but he was forced to flee in 1753 when some French Indians attacked a group of Virginia traders at the village. The village was abandoned in 1754 after the fall of Fort Necessity, and the inhabitants apparently joined the Shawnee in Ohio, though some may have joined the Cherokee in eastern Tennessee.

There may have been a settlement in eastern Kentucky in the period after the French and Indian War. Jillson places a Shawnee village at the confluence of Big Mud Lick and Little Mud Lick creeks in northern Johnson County from 1764 to 1774. This is the village from which Jenny Wiley is supposed to have made her escape. There are other references to the Shawnee in the vicinity of Big Sandy River as well. One of the most interesting accounts is the tradition of John Swift, who is said to have discovered and worked silver mines with Shawnee

CATHECASSA, Black Hoof
Artist unknown

17

laborers in eastern Kentucky from 1760 to 1770. This tradition persisted among the Shawnee as late as 1870, when a descendant of Cornstalk returned to Mud Lick Creek in Johnson County in search of silver.

It is not certain whether many of the settlements in eastern Kentucky were permanent or whether they were merely seasonal hunting or warring encampments. The Big Sandy was traveled by both the Catawba and the Shawnee when they made war on each other. During the Revolution and later the Shawnee established camps in eastern Kentucky and Tennessee from which they raided American settlers.

Long before the Cumberland Shawnee were affected by either British or French influence, they had established trading ties with the Spanish. It is probable that these ties induced some of the bands who had early settled in the Cumberland region to migrate to South Carolina, where they became known as the Savannah Indians. It is not certain exactly when the Shawnee first appeared in the Carolina region. They undoubtedly entered through the Cumberland Gap along the much used and well-known Great Warriors Path, which led from the Ohio River, south through Kentucky, through Cherokee country along the back side of the Carolinas, across Georgia, and eventually into Florida. The earliest known villages of the Shawnee in Carolina were along the headwaters of the streams and rivers flowing to the Atlantic.

The Shawnee appearance in South Carolina was fortunate for the new colony. The Westo Indians were raiding colonists in the more remote areas. Unable to handle the Westos by themselves, the struggling colonists engaged the Shawnee, who by 1680 had a considerable group in the area, to attack the Westos and bring them to Charles Town for the slave trade. By fighting the Westos the Shawnee acted as a buffer for the colonists and gained an important trade outlet for themselves, which included, among other things, the sale of slaves. In 1693 twenty Cherokee chiefs visited Charles Town to complain to Governor Thomas Smith of attacks by the Catawba, Congaree, and Shawnee, who made slave raids upon them.

There is good evidence to support the belief that the Saluda Indians, situated on the Saluda River in central South Carolina, were also Shawnee. The Saluda occupied this area from approximately 1695 to 1712, when they moved to the Conestoga River in Pennsylvania.

Beginning in the early part of the 1700s the Shawnee in South Carolina were engaged in almost constant warfare with the Catawba Indians located on the Catawba River, which divides the two Carolinas. These two tribes continued their hostilities until nearly the time of the Revolution. Because of their losses at the hands of the Catawba, the Shawnee were eventually forced to abandon their country on the Savannah River.

However, there had been a steady outmigration from South Carolina long before the trouble with the Catawba began. In 1677 or 1678 a group of approximately seventy families left Carolina and made their way north, settling near the Conestoga Indians on the Susquehanna River by 1701. It is perhaps this group which settled for some time in the vicinity of Winchester, Virginia. Other groups may have left South Carolina prior to 1707, for in addition to several villages in the vicinity of Winchester, there are Shawnee sites in Hardy County, West Virginia; Shenandoah County, Virginia; and Oldtown, Maryland, all of which date from this period.

Virginia was more than a stopover for the Shawnee. They occupied several villages in western Virginia before 1700, some for as long as twenty-five years. One village, Shawnee Springs near Winchester, was settled about 1690; and, though many of its inhabitants eventually left for Pennsylvania, a small band remained until as late as 1754. Another small village, at the mouth of the Shenandoah, was occupied well into the eighteenth century.

Apparently the Shawnee's withdrawal from South Carolina annoyed the white government, which found them useful as a bulwark against other tribes and, what was probably more important, as slave traders. In 1711 the commissioners of the Indian trade expressed their concern regarding Shawnee migration, instructing their agents to prevent them from leaving.

Strong circumstantial evidence confirms that in spite of all the government's attempts the Savannah in question did, after all, desert.

The Yamasee War in 1715 found at least some of the Shawnee involved in opposition to the Carolina government. The struggle was basically a quarrel between the South Carolina colony and the Spanish colony in Florida, but most of the actual fighting was done by the various Indian tribes aligned with the respective colonies. As a result of the war, at least one band of Shawnee fled to the Chattahoochee River, which separates Georgia from Alabama, and settled near the present city of Fort Gaines, Georgia. Here they were joined by a band of Yuchi, who accompanied them to the Tallapoosa River in 1733. A band of about thirty Shawnee was still on the Savannah River in 1725, and it has been suggested that they may have been the Hathawekela who were reported in Pennsylvania in 1731.

This latter band was the last recorded group of Shawnee in the Carolina region for nearly twenty years. About 1750 a mixed band of Shawnee and Seneca from western Pennsylvania settled near Keowee, a lower Cherokee town in western South Carolina. From this location they proceeded to raid the Catawba and annoy the back settlements of South Carolina.

Alabama was a favored location for many Shawnee bands either as a temporary or permanent settlement. It is probable that bands of Shawnee found their way to Alabama from the Cumberland region during or even before the seventeenth-century conflict with the Iroquois. There is good evidence that intimate ties were established between a band of Shawnee and the Tukabatchee Creek prior to 1685. Governor Nicholson of South Carolina, in a letter to the Carolina Board of Trade, August 20, 1698, said that he had an account from some "Chaouanon" Indians whose country lay southwest of South Carolina. They were accompanied by a Frenchman who had been with La Salle when he was killed.

Another band came to Alabama after fleeing the Chattahoochee River in South Carolina as a result of the Yamasee

War in 1715. This band migrated to the Tallapoosa River and may have been the inhabitants of a village called Ikanhatki. And in 1747 a sizable band of Shawnee from the Ohio River established a village or villages along the upper reaches of the Coosa River, midway between the Upper Creeks and the Cherokee. This band was led by Peter Chartier, a French trader whose father had married a Shawnee woman. By 1748 a village, Chalakagay, was established near the present site of Sylacauga in Talladega County near the Abihka Indians. These Shawnee were joined by others from the north, and several villages were established in the Abihka country. Chartier left this region for the Cumberland River in 1755. Apparently many of his group remained in Alabama, however, for there were still Shawnee in the Abihka country in 1757. At the time of their arrival in Alabama, Chartier's group numbered 450, but when they were driven from the vicinity of Nashville by the Chickasaw in 1756, their number totaled only about 270; at least a portion of the group had probably stayed on in Alabama.

The settlements along the Tallapoosa appear to have been somewhat permanent. A number of references list Shawnee villages in this vicinity from 1760 to 1799. The Revolution drove other Shawnee to take refuge with the Creeks, and in 1791 they had four villages in the Montgomery area along the Tallapoosa and upper Alabama rivers. Following the Creek War of 1814 the Shawnee gradually abandoned the state. It is not recorded where they went, but they very likely migrated to Missouri and formed a part of the Absentee Shawnee (so called because of their absence during the treaty which took their Missouri land), whose recent ties to the Creek Indians seem to be stronger than those of other Shawnee groups.

By the latter part of the seventeenth century bands of Shawnee were making their way toward Pennsylvania from at least three general locations: South Carolina, the Cumberland region, and Illinois. The date the first band entered Pennsylvania is uncertain. It is known that the inhabitants of at least one village abandoned South Carolina in 1677 or 1678 and migrated north. There is no direct evidence of Shawnee settlement in Pennsylvania, however, until 1692.

As early as 1691 the representatives of Albany and Esopus had urged upon the New York General Assembly that communications and peace be made with the Indians to the west, with the view of increasing the fur and peltry business. Led by Arant Vielle, representatives spent fifteen months in Shawnee country, undoubtedly in the Cumberland region; and in 1694 the party returned with about 700 Shawnee. This large group established the village of Pechoquealin on the Delaware River where today we find the town of Shawnee-on-Delaware.

In 1697 or 1698 about seventy families of Shawnee settled on the Susquehanna near the Conestoga Indians and built a village called Pequea at the mouth of a creek by that same name in Lancaster County. Between 1697 and 1728 several Shawnee villages were built along the Susquehanna and on Pequea Creek and from this creek north to the Juniata River, with one village, called Chillisquaque, on the west bank of the Susquehanna as far north as present-day Sunbury in Northumberland County.

With the death of William Penn in 1717 relations between the Shawnee and the Pennsylvania government began to deteriorate, and by 1727 many of the Shawnee bands were ready to migrate west, following some of the Delaware who had begun this westward movement in 1722. The towns on the Delaware River were abandoned in 1728. The Shawnee on Chillisquaque Creek moved to the western part of the state in 1728 as well. These groups were followed from 1732 to 1734 by the greater part of the Pequea Shawnee from the lower Susquehanna River. Only a few Shawnee remained in the eastern part of Pennsylvania.

Attempts by the Pennsylvania government to attract the Shawnee back to the eastern section failed. The Iroquois, who were given protectorate rights over the other Indian tribes of the colony, were actively used by the government to encourage the Shawnee to return. But it is apparent that the Shawnee, though previously tolerant of this arrangement, were no longer willing to accept Iroquois domination.

As the Pennsylvania Shawnee began to migrate west around 1730, some may have moved beyond the boundary of Pennsylvania into Ohio. After murdering a Mingo chief, one band of Shawnee fled westward. Where they went is uncertain, but it is probable that they fled down the Ohio as far as the Scioto River, where a town was established in 1734. The Shawnee were breaking away, not only from the influence of the English, but also from the authority of the Iroquois.

Logstown, on the Ohio River about eighteen miles below Fort Duquesne (the present site of Pittsburgh), was occupied by Seneca, Shawnee, and Delaware, and the town was a major trading center for Pennsylvania until the mid 1750s. After the fall of Fort Duquesne to the British in 1758, Logstown was abandoned and the Shawnee there moved to Ohio. By this time most of the Shawnee had left Pennsylvania and by the end of the French and Indian War there were no longer any of them left in the state.

During the French and Indian War most of the Shawnee were located along the upper Ohio River in Pennsylvania and what is now Ohio, from the Allegheny River to the Scioto. However, there were bands of Shawnee in Virginia, Alabama, Kentucky, and probably on the lower Ohio River as well.

The first major Shawnee village west of Pennsylvania on the Ohio River was Lower Shawnee Town, situated at the mouth of the Scioto River across from present-day Portsmouth, Ohio. Its advantageous location on both the Ohio River and the Great Warriors Path made it a favorite rendezvous for the Shawnee and an important center for French and English fur traders. It was apparently established between 1729 and 1739. Explorer Christopher Gist in 1751 reported a considerable settlement of about 300 men living in some forty houses on the Kentucky side of the Ohio and one hundred houses on the north side. In 1753 a flood destroyed the village, driving the inhabitants across the Scioto to the higher ground on which Portsmouth was afterwards built. The latter site was abandoned in 1758, and the Indians living there moved to the upper Scioto and the Little Miami rivers.

The Shawnee from Pennsylvania built several towns in what

is today eastern Ohio, along the Ohio River and on or near the Muskingum River. The town of Waketameki was the largest and most important Shawnee village on the Muskingum, located near present-day Dresden, Ohio, in Muskingum County.

When Lower Shawnee Town was abandoned in 1758, the majority of its inhabitants moved up the Scioto and reestablished their village on the plains four miles below the present city of Circleville. This became known as Chillicothe, one of five villages of that name in Ohio. Two other Chillicothe villages were located further downriver, one at the city in Ross County which still bears that name and another on the north fork of Paint Creek, also in Ross County.

After a peace treaty with Colonel Henry Bouquet in 1764, those of the Shawnee on the Scioto and Muskingum who signed the treaty migrated westward and established two villages on the Little Miami and Mad rivers. The town that became known as "Old Chillicothe" was built on the Little Miami River, three miles north of the present city of Xenia, Ohio. This village became famous as the place where Daniel Boone and Simon Kenton were held captive. About twelve miles north of it stood the town of Piqua on the north bank of Mad River. Most biographers believe that Piqua was the birthplace of Tecumseh. Both of these villages were destroyed in 1780 by an expedition from Kentucky, under the command of George Rogers Clark. The residents then retired to a fifth Chillicothe, on the Great Miami River.

It was against these villages in western Ohio that much of the activity of the Kentucky militia was focused. From the period of the Revolution the Shawnee in this area opposed white settlement and established an alliance of western tribes to resist it actively. The Indians' spirit was broken, however, by the force led by General Anthony Wayne at Fallen Timbers in 1794. As a result of the subsequent Treaty of Greenville, in 1795, Piqua was abandoned. The largest body of its inhabitants migrated north to Wapakoneta on the Auglaize River in Ohio.

A Shawnee named Lewis, who attached himself to the service of the United States in the War of 1812, fighting against Tecumseh at the Battle of the Thames, became the head of a village, today called Lewistown, situated on Stony Creek in Logan County, Ohio, just to the east of Wapakoneta. In 1817 the Shawnee received their first title to land from the United States government for their settlements at Wapakoneta and at Hog Creek, where Lima, Ohio, now stands.

Long before Andrew Jackson wrote one of the most inhumane chapters in American history by his manner of removing the Indians from east of the Mississippi River, many Shawnee had already voluntarily migrated west of the Father of Waters. Some may have settled in Missouri as early as 1763.

With the purchase of Louisiana by the United States in 1803, the idea of Indian removal was first officially expressed by Thomas Jefferson. Though the policy was never fully acted upon until Jackson became president, the eastern Indians were encouraged, and indeed pressured, to migrate to this new American acquisition. By 1815 there were some 1,200 Shawnee residing in towns along Apple Creek, near Cape Girardeau, and on the Merrimack River, near Saint Louis, and a census report in 1822 listed 1,383 Shawnee in Missouri.

As Shawnee continued to arrive in Missouri from east of the Mississippi, a large band of Delaware and the Absentee Shawnee moved south into Arkansas and eventually located in Texas. About 300 Shawnee families arrived in Texas in 1820.

In 1825 a treaty with the Missouri Indians ceded all the land around Cape Girardeau to the United States. In return the Shawnee were given a tract in southwestern Missouri. As this site was not acceptable, they chose instead a tract on the Kansas River.

With the election of Andrew Jackson to the presidency in 1828, the fate of those Shawnee who had chosen to remain in Ohio was sealed. Migration west was no longer voluntary but the result of a relentless policy of the new administration. In September of 1832, after much delay due in part to the inept leadership of the Indian agent, the Wapakoneta Shawnee left. In the summer of 1833 the Hog Creek Shawnee removed to

QUATAWAPEA, Colonel Lewis
Painted by Charles Bird King
From Thomas L. McKenney and James Hall, *History of the
Indian Tribes of North America* (Philadelphia, 1842)

Kansas. For the first time in their history there were no Shawnee east of the Mississippi River. The seemingly unlimited resources of the Eastern Woodlands were being taken over by white settlers.

By 1867 the Shawnee were located on three reservations in Indian Territory, now Oklahoma. The Absentee Shawnee from Texas were settled with the Potawatomi in what is today Pottawatomie County. The Kansas Shawnee migrated to the Cherokee reservation in 1867 and in 1870 were incorporated with the Cherokee Nation. A mixed band of Seneca and Shawnee settled in Ottawa County, Oklahoma. After centuries of migration there was no longer anywhere else to go. The Shawnee are still to be found in these locations.

3

SOCIAL ORGANIZATION

DURING THE late prehistoric period the Central Algonquians who lived in the Ohio Valley evolved a culture based on agriculture and centered on the village, the major ceremonial, political, and economic unit, to which lineage units were subordinate. This pattern remained characteristic of the Shawnee well into the twentieth century.

If one accepts the traditional definition of the clan as a unilineal kinship group that maintains the fiction of common genetic descent from a remote ancestor, usually legendary or mythological, then it is questionable whether the Shawnee actually had a clan system. Clans among other Algonquian tribes seldom numbered more than twelve, but Tenskwautawa, the Shawnee Prophet and brother of Tecumseh, mentioned thirty-four totemic names for the Shawnee, suggesting that these belonged to individual families, not clans.

Since only twelve of these names were still being used in 1824 when Tenskwautawa was interviewed, it is possible that the totemic units were no longer family groups. In 1859 the Shawnee had essentially thirteen nonlineal name groups. In 1935 it was discovered that they had a social organization that embraced many of the features characteristic of a clan system but lacked the clan units. In their place the Shawnee had six name groups with totemic names. These were: Turkey, representing bird life; Turtle, aquatic life; Rounded-feet, carnivores; Horse, hoofed animals; Raccoon, animals with paws;

and Rabbit, a peaceful nature. At birth a child was given a name by a family-designated name-giver. If the name assigned to an individual was wrong, usually indicated by sickness, the name could be changed to place him in a group more reflective of his nature. A special relationship between name groups existed. Specified pairs of name groups buried one another's dead, for instance. And specific functions might be assigned to a particular name group. The Turtle, for example, normally carried the sacred bundle (a package of ritual paraphernalia) because he moves slowly and carefully. But name groups functioned primarily as friendship groups and were the basis for joking relationships. Other functions and characteristics normally assigned to clans—blood revenge, mythological ancestry, and unilateral descent—were absent.

The village band was more important for the Shawnee than the lineage or name group. The organization of ritual, appointment of ritual offices, and naming of custodians of the sacred bundle were duties of the village chief. New ceremonies might originate in an individual totemic vision and could be incorporated into village patterns. Totemic visions were sought during shamanistic or puberty ceremony trances. Thus the village, not the name group, was the ritual unit, and ceremonial organization cut across the totemic system. The cycle of ritual correlated with the summer occupation of the village, and the village also functioned as the economic unit.

Apparently *societies* (secret men's clubs common in many Algonquian tribes) were not a part of the organizational make-up of the Shawnee. Both Tenskwautawa and Black Hoof mentioned the "Miseekwaaweekwaakee," which corresponds to the Man Eaters of the Miami and Kickapoo. Somewhat like a military society, this group supposedly ceremonially feasted on the bodies of war captives. But it was unlike a military society in that membership was inherited and the group was headed by four women. Though Black Hoof knew in 1825 of descendants of members of the society, he supposed that the duties of their profession had not been carried out for many years.

Traditionally marriages were arranged by the mother's

brother, and marriage of relatives was forbidden. Sororal polygyny was common, with the obligation of a man to marry the widow of a brother being strictly enforced. Even in the earliest records the household was basically a nuclear family of a mother, father, and their children. Family ties among the Shawnee beyond this were not strong and there was a narrow range of kin ties (which did include the grandparents), pointing again to the village rather than the family as the basic organizational unit of the Shawnee. Because of the practice of sororal polygyny, the role of adoption was relatively minor for the Shawnee. There are no records of intratribal ceremonial adoption. There are records, however, of white captives being adopted into Shawnee families.

The family was important for the Shawnee, particularly in the training of the children. This process began very early in life and concentrated on those things that would be necessary for success as adult Shawnee. From the beginning babies were strapped to a cradle board to insure that they would grow straight and strong. Even the head was bound to the board, a practice that produced a flat spot on the back of the head characteristic of all Shawnee until recent times. To make the infants hardy they were bathed every morning, winter and summer, in cold water. The games of the children were designed to develop strength and resourcefulness. Bows and arrows were made for boys, and a rolling hoop made from a wild grapevine was used as a target. Running, swimming, and jumping were everyday activities, teaching agility and developing strength.

The young were taught early to respect older persons, and from the aged grandparents came much of the education for the young. Boys were taught hunting, fishing, and trapping, as well as the arts of war and discipline. Although this was done as play, it was serious business. These were skills essential to survival and as important to the Shawnee as school was to white children. Boys and girls alike were drilled in the tradition and history of the Shawnee people, developing both a knowledge of the past and the skill of oratory.

Slavery was not widely practiced by the Shawnee, even

though they were involved in the slaving business in South Carolina for a short time. Black captives were found among the Shawnee, but they were assimilated into Shawnee culture and often served as interpreters. Some captives, male and female, appeared to have been enslaved, but the tasks assigned them were basically those of the Shawnee women.

The organization of Shawnee subsistence activities was not very different from that of most groups in the Eastern Woodlands. Hunting was the principal occupation of the men. The women of the tribe did much of the mundane work around the settlement, such as planting and cultivating corn, dressing game, and even building houses. The men assisted the women to some extent in raising corn, but farming was primarily a woman's occupation. Men helped the women prepare the field by cutting brush and grubbing out roots and sometimes helped with the harvest, but most of the gathering and all the preparation of the corn for eating was done by the women.

The economic cycle resembled the usual Central Algonquian seasonal pattern in its emphasis on hunting and agriculture. In the summer the Shawnee occupied semipermanent villages along rivers, and the women tended nearby fields while the men hunted in the vicinity. Their winter activities, however, were different from the other Central Algonquian groups. Travelers and traders often record finding the Shawnee villages abandoned during the winter months. During this season the Shawnee broke up into small family bands. In the winter camps the women were often employed in making maple sugar while the men were away on extended hunts.

No specific information regarding the rights of land tenure for the Shawnee hunting territory exists. Their frequent migrations would have made hereditary territorial rights meaningless. In most cases hunting rights were controlled by other tribes occupying the territory into which the Shawnee migrated, and the use of these territories was negotiated by the various Shawnee divisions or bands. Present-day Kentucky was used extensively as a hunting territory by the Shawnee.

Although there was no private ownership of cultivated lands, a woman controlled the crops planted in her patch.

There was much cooperation among the village women, and tending crops was a social as well as an economic function. A woman seldom worked alone in her field, but she alone had absolute rights to its products. Even her husband was required to give a gift if he wanted a few ears of corn for some ceremonial purpose. From the woman's view the corn was to be used to feed her family, and she would not trade it away for something she wanted for herself.

The presence of European traders meant that the Shawnee became increasingly dependent upon trade for basic non-perishable items. Accounts of trading are numerous, but little is known of the organization of this trade within the Shawnee culture. The heavy reliance on skins and furs as goods to be traded suggests that most Shawnee hunters spent a significant portion of their time accumulating these items. It was common practice for European traders to establish trade relations by giving the village chiefs presents. This suggests that trade was controlled by the village headmen who acted for the entire community. But some trade with individuals may have taken place; there are accounts of traders encountering bands of Shawnee hunters returning from hunting trips and relieving them of their furs for a few kegs of whiskey. This practice usually met with protests from the Shawnee, however, and colonial governments attempted to discourage it.

There is some indication that the Shawnee may have been salt traders. Numerous references to salt-making exist, and a few imply a salt-trading role for the Shawnee. But with whom they traded, if they did so, is not certain.

Shawnee political organization was more complex, formal, and structured than that of other Algonquian groups. Its unique feature was the importance of the five major divisions. These divisions may have been the principal villages at a time when the Shawnee were all occupying a common territory, although they have been called a variety of things, including clans. In historic times their structure and function is not entirely clear. It is apparent that entire villages identified themselves with a single major division and that the divisions served in some political, religious, and military division of labor. Each division seems to have been responsible for a particular kind of activity related to tribal welfare. The Chillicothe division was responsible for supplying the tribal chief. While Thomas Wildcat Alford, a college-educated Shawnee, indicates that the function of the Mequachake division concerned health and medicine, other sources suggest that this division supplied the priests, a function Alford ascribes to the Piqua division. All sources agree that the Kispogogi were the warriors, but Tenskwautawa said that the head of the warriors was a Piqua. Little is known of the Hathawekela, and Alford includes them with the Chillicothe as being concerned with political matters.

Although each division was responsible for some specific function within the Shawnee organization as a whole, each was also an autonomous political unit. In historic times each had its own chief and often its own affiliations with other tribes. Each division also had a subculture which in certain minor aspects differed from that of any other. The Mequachake, for example, shared certain feasts and ceremonies with the Creek Indians not practiced by the other divisions.

It is possible that the Shawnee were disrupted by the Iroquois in the mid-seventeenth century before a stronger tribal identity could be established. But their conservatism in other matters suggests that the Shawnee were slow to give up established patterns and probably fairly represent an earlier stage of Algonquian social and political organization.

According to tradition the tribal chief of the Shawnee was to come from the Chillicothe division. But in historic times chiefs were normally spoken of in the plural, indicating the headmen of the various divisions and bands. Their role as chief was patrilineally inherited, though primogeniture was not the rule. Tenskwautawa said that when an old chief died, the new one was appointed or recognized by the surviving village chiefs and the principal men without respect to his age. If no son was left to inherit the title, it did not descend to any other relative to the exclusion of fit persons not related to the deceased.

The dual system of peace chiefs and war chiefs at the village level, common throughout the East, was also practiced by the

Shawnee. While the office of peace or village chief was apparently hereditary, the position of war chief was earned and represented a reward for talents and bravery. As the economy became dominated by government annuity payments (yearly recompense for lands taken by the whites) and controlled by white traders, positions of authority were easily taken over by a new type of self-made chief who first overshadowed and then, with the help of traders and white governmental officials, replaced hereditary chiefs. Some of the Shawnee bands resisted this development, and their war chiefs commanded the highest respect and loyalty.

Tecumseh is a good example of a war chief and was most aggressive in resisting white settlement and influence. He was born in 1768 in Ohio and grew to be a very striking man. Some sources say he was nearly six feet tall, much taller than most Shawnee. Very early he gained a reputation as a fighter and led many raids into Kentucky against white settlements. Tecumseh was also an eloquent speaker and often served as the spokesman for the Shawnee at councils between white officials and the tribes in the Ohio Valley. He was not a hereditary chief, but his prowess at fighting attracted a loyal following. While Black Hoof and most of the other Shawnee made their peace with the white government after the Treaty of Greenville in 1795, Tecumseh and his band continued to resist from their settlements on the White River in Indiana and later along Tippecanoe Creek. Actually Tecumseh's band was comprised of people from various tribal groups in the upper Ohio Valley, including Miami, Wyandot, Delaware, Kickapoo, Potawatomi, and others. He spent much of his time traveling in the Ohio Valley and in the South trying to rally other Indian groups to his cause, but with little success. His resistance continued until the War of 1812, when he was made a general in the British army and led the contingent of Indians in the capture of Detroit. Had the British soldiers and leaders fought as well and as bravely as the Indians under the leadership of Tecumseh, the outcome in the West might have been different. But with the British in retreat the army was attacked by a force led by General William Henry Harrison on the

TECUMSEH
Courtesy, Smithsonian Institution,
National Anthropological Archives

Thames River in Ontario, and in this battle on October 5, 1813, Tecumseh was killed. After that, his brother Tenskwautawa and his followers gave up the fight.

Peculiar to the Shawnee and Miami was the tradition of women chiefs. These were often close relatives of the principal chiefs, and like them they were separated according to peace and war functions. Apparently they were a kind of women's auxiliary, but they held a great deal of power and their decisions on questions of peace and war carried equal weight with those of the male chiefs. They also functioned as superintendents of female affairs in the village, particularly women's activities during ceremonies and feasts. A few women also sat in the councils of the Shawnee, and widows occasionally served as interim chiefs until successors to their husbands could be chosen.

The councils were important in that decisions were often arrived at by consensus. Peace chiefs, in reality, made few decisions on their own and exercised little authority in most matters. War chiefs held their own councils, but the nature of their decisions gave them relatively more power than the peace chiefs had.

Law for the Shawnee was largely a private matter. Most infractions, from petty theft to murder, were normally handled by the accused and the accuser or their families. Often wrongs were atoned by feasts and presents in proportion to the nature of the offense and the rank and sex of the injured party. For example, the Shawnee paid double for killing a woman because she could raise children. Although reparations normally took the form of gifts or money, corporal and even capital punishment was known, particularly in cases of adultery or murder. When the village or tribe was affected by murder or other offenses, or when the case could not be solved privately, the family would consult the tribe for a resolution of the problem.

Crimes against the village were rare; one's first allegiance was to his community. Wrongs against another person did occur, but rarely if the perpetrator was sober. If he was drunk, his actions were often forgiven on the theory that the drink, and not the man, had occasioned the abuse. The law itself was not codified but was based on principles of morality and honesty. As was true of most American Indian tribes, these concepts of morality did not extend beyond the tribe and especially not to whites. Cunning and deception were ways of coping with whites, whom the Shawnee perceived as being equally deceitful toward them.

4

SUBSISTENCE AND TECHNOLOGY

SUBSISTENCE ACTIVITIES were governed by a seasonal cycle. At the end of September the families began to leave the main village to begin the winter hunt. Some of the winter months were spent in trapping, an activity that became more important as the Shawnee became increasingly dependent upon the fur trade. In March the various families began to return to the main village, and in April and May fields were cleared for planting. During the summer months the women tended the crops and gathered wild plant food, while the men spent the time hunting or fishing occasionally as the need arose.

The seasons were marked by annual ceremonies. The first of these occurred usually in April and was called the Bread Dance or le Feu Nouveau (the New Fire). The dance itself was preceded by a ceremonial ball game played between the men and women, and the twenty kernels of corn used in scoring were planted by one of the women chiefs, after which all the corn could be planted. Another ceremony occurred at harvest and was called Fête du Petit Blé (Feast of Small Grain). A Green Corn Ceremony, probably borrowed from the Creek Indians, was held by the Shawnee in August.

That all these ceremonies were concerned with agricultural activities would seem to indicate that a significant degree of importance was attached to agriculture. There were no corresponding ceremonies regarding the hunt, but this was probably because during the hunting season the tribe or villages were split into family units too small for community ceremonial activities. There was comparative leisure among the Shawnee because the simple life they lived did not demand continual effort to provide necessities. This would suggest that hunting was the dominant and preferred mode of subsistence.

Hunting and trapping were important activities not only for subsistence but also to supply the Shawnee with skins and furs for use in trade. It is not known whether hunting was a year-round activity for the Shawnee before the arrival of the European fur-trader, but afterwards, except for some subsistence hunting in the summer, hunting and trapping were confined to the late fall and winter months when the pelts of fur-bearing animals were of better quality.

During the extended hunts animals that were killed would be hung in trees until the hunter could return and take them back to the winter camp. Other hunters never molested game stored in this fashion and marked by the owner. The only worry was that buzzards and other vermin might eat it.

Buffalo, deer, and turkey were preferred food animals, but almost any other kind of animal, including wildcats, would be eaten. Deerskins were also an important trade item, and when the deer began to lose their winter coats Shawnee men devoted more time to trapping raccoon, beaver, and other fur-bearing creatures.

Buffalo were a favored prey of the Shawnee. Although the herds did not compare in size to those found on the Great Plains, relatively large numbers of buffalo existed in most of the regions occupied by the Shawnee east of the Mississippi. The only exceptions were Alabama and extreme eastern Pennsylvania. Herds in the Carolinas, western Pennsylvania, Ohio, and Kentucky were described as large, although not so large that the Indians would waste any of the carcass. Most of the meat was eaten, the hides were made into robes, and even the bones were used for implements. Some robes were traded, but the buffalo did not exist in sufficient numbers in the East to be a major trade item. As European civilization advanced westward, the buffalo became extinct. By 1800 they were nearly extinct in Kentucky and the Ohio Valley.

Deer were an important food source and their skins a significant trade item for the Shawnee. Unlike the buffalo, the deer were not threatened immediately by the advancing civilization. In fact, the settlers' clearings and grain crops served to increase the deer population. Along the heavily peopled East Coast, herds did begin to decline before the end of the colonial period, but in the Ohio Valley deerskins remained a major trade item for the Shawnee into the nineteenth century.

Fishing was used to supplement the diet during the summer months. The importance of fishing depended on location and the availability of other food resources. Four different methods were used for catching fish: angling, trapping with wicker traps, netting, and spearing from canoes.

Farming in the Eastern Woodlands was an arduous activity. The first job was to clear the land of trees and brush, a considerable job in this region, particularly before steel axes, spades, and hoes were available. Fire was extensively used for clearing. The rich woodland soil proved troublesome for the women, for besides crops it also produced an abundance of weeds.

The Shawnee women planted several varieties of corn, including a red corn, a dark blue corn, a soft white corn, and a hard white or "glass" corn, each of which had a special use. Kernels to be planted were coated with grease or dipped in water in which fish bones had been soaked. No attention was paid to phases of the moon, but corn, beans, and squash were planted early in the morning. Corn was planted in hills about four feet apart, and the hills were in rows about three feet apart oriented in an east-west direction. Irrigation was not practiced, and the only fertilizer used was the ash left on the ground after clearing. Beans, gourds, pumpkins, squash, and sunflowers were also included in the patch, and in the more southerly areas sweet potatoes were raised. In Virginia even tobacco was noted. (It is not known whether the Shawnee ever raised tobacco in Kentucky.)

Although the Shawnee have been classified as corn agriculturalists, the crop was not a year-round staple for them. This would have required about one acre per person, and the Shawnee cultivated only from one-half to one acre for a family of four or more—that is, about one-eighth to one-fourth acre for each person. An example of the lack of dependency on agriculture can be seen in the failure of the Kentuckians' attempt to weaken the Shawnee in Ohio by destroying their villages and cornfields.

The Quaker mission at Wapakoneta in the early nineteenth century was effective in producing changes in agriculture for some of Black Hoof's group. By 1830 the Quakers had managed to introduce new farming practices with individual farmers. Livestock was introduced, and a few of the men began to be involved in full-scale subsistence farming. This carried over to their reservations in Kansas and Oklahoma. Eventually lack of hunting grounds forced many to turn to these practices.

Although collecting wild foods was not a major subsistence activity of the Shawnee, it did add variety to the diet, and it became important when crops were poor or were destroyed. Herbs were collected and dried for use in seasoning meat. One root, used during travel, resembled ginger in appearance and had a warm and pleasant taste. Other wild plants collected by the Shawnee included wild potato, wild onion, milkweed, and a number of varieties of nuts. Two other roots used were the man of the earth (perhaps ginseng), and the Jerusalem artichoke. In season, abundant use was made of wild fruits, including strawberries, dewberries, blackberries, cherries, plums, and grapes. Pawpaws were abundant in some localities, as were huckleberries and even persimmons. Fruits that could be dried were highly valued, and the persimmon, when seeded and cored, was dried and made into a cake called persimmon bread. Other fruits such as plums and berries were dried and reconstituted when needed by cooking in water.

There were many salt springs or licks in Kentucky, and making salt was a major extractive industry for the Shawnee. Originally salt was made by evaporating the salt-laden water in large clay vessels or salt pans, leaving a thin residue of salt. Later, iron kettles were used in place of the clay pans. Summer or early fall was apparently the usual time for the activity, which occupied several days. Making maple sugar was also an important yearly activity. When the sap began to flow, about February, the women collected the sap, boiled it in large kettles, and poured it into wooden dishes to cool and granulate. Although it was a women's activity, men were known to have been involved in it in later times, and captives were often employed in the work. The lack of natural resources eliminated the making of salt and sugar after the Shawnee moved to Oklahoma.

The Shawnee prepared their food in much the same way as most other woodland tribes. Cooking was usually done out of doors. Meat was roasted, boiled, or fried in bear's grease. It was normally eaten fresh but was occasionally smoked and dried, particularly for use while traveling. Corn was prepared in a number of ways depending on variety and intended use. It was roasted for future use, and boiled with meat or other vegetables when needed. Breads could be made from the soft, milky mush of fresh corn, from flour of beaten parched corn, or from a meal mixed with ashes to produce a heavy bluish-colored dough. Hominy was made by boiling matured corn in a mixture of water and wood ashes, and some corn was even fermented to be made into a type of beer drunk on special occasions and offered to guests. The interesting aspect of Shawnee food preparation is that the practices described in 1934 do not differ from those mentioned in the eighteenth and early nineteenth centuries.

The area of Shawnee culture most influenced by Europeans was undoubtedly technology. Many areas of native skill virtually disappeared. Guns had early replaced the bow and arrow; metal pots had replaced pottery; and some of the clothing and ornaments were of European weave or manufacture. Still, many traditional items of native manufacture were used, either because they were unavailable from white traders or because of preference. Housing was one item that resisted change.

Unlike the Plains Indians, who could dismantle their dwellings and take their housing with them, the Shawnee built permanent structures that had to be left behind. It might be expected that a people who moved as often as the Shawnee would adopt movable houses similar to the teepee used by the Indians on the Western Plains. But conditions in the Eastern Woodlands differed from those in the Plains in several respects. Unlike the Plains, the Woodlands offered an abundant supply of materials for houses, a circumstance making it unnecessary to transport such materials from place to place. And it would have been impossible to drag a travois over the woodland trails, even if the Shawnee had used dogs or horses for this purpose. Therefore it was more practical for the Shawnee to abandon their houses and build new ones at their new location.

Shawnee houses were single-family dwellings, easily constructed in a few days and abandoned with little concern. The Shawnee wigwam or wegiwa was square or oblong in shape, and the dimensions were determined by the size of the family. One house described by a captive was about twenty feet long by fourteen feet wide. About the height of a man at the center, the Shawnee wigwam had a pitched roof and vertical sides. The construction of the wigwam has been most thoroughly described by Thomas Wildcat Alford in his book *Civilization:*

In building a wegiwa the bark was obtained by first severing it from the body of a tree as it stood, mostly from elm and birch. . . . the bark was laid flat on level ground, with flesh side under, weighted down with small logs, and allowed to dry to a certain extent, but used while still soft and pliable. Then poles were cut of straight young trees and set into the ground at regular distances apart, outlining the size desired for the wegiwa. All bark was peeled off the poles to keep worms from working in it. Two of these poles with a fork at the top of each were set at opposite ends and at half way the length of the wegiwa. Upon these forks were laid the ends of a long pole . . . tied securely with rough bark. This formed the top comb of the roof, to which the rest of the poles were bent to a suitable height for the walls and firmly secured there with strips of bark. Then upon and across

SHAWNEE HOUSE, sketched by the author

these were laid other poles at regular distances from the top comb, down the slope to the end of the roof, and on down the sides to form the walls. Upon these cross poles were laid the sheets of bark . . . securely held in place by other poles laid on the outside of the bark and tied fast to the poles within. The work seems intricate . . . but to a dexterous Indian woman . . . it was easily and quickly done.

Sometimes platform beds, tables, shelves, and benches were constructed inside the wigwam. The structures were waterproof and provided a comfortable dwelling even in cold weather. Since the bark could be easily removed from the tree only in the spring, hides of animals were often substituted in houses constructed at other times of the year.

Besides individual homes, the larger and more permanent Shawnee villages also contained a council house called a msikamekwi. These were much larger structures, used for ceremonies and secular dances in addition to council meetings. The explorer Christopher Gist described the "statehouse" at Lower Shawnee Town at the mouth of the Scioto River as being about ninety feet long. The council house at Greenville, Ohio, was a frame structure 150 feet by 34 feet in size. This building formed the nucleus of the community and was constructed cooperatively by the entire village.

Clothing of European weave was worn, but it was slow in replacing dressed skins for regular use. Although there are accounts of men preparing skins, this was normally an activity of the women. Deer hide was the most common material used in clothing. But before the extinction of the buffalo east of the Mississippi, the hide of this animal was made into winter robes and the thin belly skin was tanned to a chamoislike softness. After the skin was stretched and the hair and fat scraped off, it was dressed with animal brains to soften it. These dressed skins were made into several articles of clothing. In the winter both sexes wore moccasins, leggings to the top of their thighs, a breech-cloth between the legs, a girdle around the waist, and a hat. Men wore a loose shirt while the women wore a longer overblouse. In the summer the men wore only a breech-cloth and the women wore a loose overblouse. Often the shirts and blouses were decorated with dyed porcupine quills, bright-colored feathers, and paints. Later as the Shawnee obtained items of European manufacture they decorated their clothing with silver trinkets and glass beads. Calico shirts gradually replaced skin shirts as the hides were increasingly needed for trade purposes.

Shawnee women were also engaged in several other craft activities. They made rope of wild hemp and wove bags for carrying food and other items. Rugs and tapestries were woven from dyed straw and feathers. Unfortunately, little is known about these activities. Once the Shawnee obtained manufactured goods from European traders, these traditional crafts were abandoned.

The making of sieves for sifting meal or separating grain into different sizes gives a clue as to the ingenuity of Shawnee basket-making, which early became a lost art. Material was obtained by cutting down a hackberry tree, stripping off the bark, and pounding the trunk until the thin layers of annual growth could be peeled off. Strips of these layers were woven into sifters of various size, and tradition has it that Shawnee women at one time could make watertight baskets in this fashion.

Other items reflect the ingenuity of the Shawnee in working with wood. The use of wooden bowls and spoons is often mentioned by captives and others who encountered the Shawnee. These were carved from the knots of hardwood trees. Henry Harvey, a missionary to the Shawnee in Ohio, describes a sophisticated system of trapping animals which kept them alive until the hunter could return to retrieve his quarry and reset the trap's triggering mechanism. The traps consisted of wooden poles placed along streams and marshes. The animals, as they crossed the poles, would trip the trigger made of deer sinew and cause other poles to fall into place trapping the quarry.

The Shawnee at Wapakoneta, Ohio, were early influenced by technological change. The Quaker mission introduced saw- and gristmills, and some of the Shawnee there began to take on the trappings of civilization. Board houses and furniture replaced the wigwams. Corn was ground at the mill, which freed the women from much labor. Carpentry was learned, and tools were accumulated with which plows, harrows, wagons, bedsteads, tables, bureaus, and other farm and household items were made. After reaching Oklahoma most of the remaining Shawnee adopted these changes.

5

IDEOLOGY AND EXPRESSIVE CULTURE

LIKE MOST OTHER non-European cultures, the Shawnee's ideology did not make a clear distinction between science and religion. Rather they were more concerned with the distinction between the normal and the abnormal. Shawnee beliefs and practices focused upon retaining or restoring conditions to a state of normalcy (the way things ought to be). Religious practices were designed to insure good crops, successful hunts, or to ward off disease. Medical practice attempted to restore a sick or injured person back to normal.

Shawnee medical practice was very much wrapped up in ideology and even witchcraft. In fact the Shawnee word for priest means "one who does the sucking," indicating a shaman who sucks evil spirits from the body. However, the Shawnee had a different word for doctor, and the word for medicine literally means root. This distinction between priest and doctor indicates that they had special practitioners involved in treating illness and injury.

Shawnee doctors had an excellent reputation and were reported to have performed feats that seemed almost magical. John Heckewelder, a Moravian missionary, noted that a Shawnee woman in half an hour cured his injured finger that white doctors had been unable to remedy. He also said that missionary women often sought Shawnee women doctors to cure complaints "peculiar to their sex." Their surgeons excelled in the curing of external wounds that were beyond the skill of white practitioners. The uses of curative roots and herbs were known by virtually all the Shawnee. The Creek Indians had an almost mystical faith in Shawnee doctors and attributed to them powers only a little less than divine.

Shawnee group ritual was organized at the village level, rather than by clans as was more typical of Algonquian groups. Certain annual feasts and dances have already been mentioned in connection with subsistence activities. Another yearly ceremony was a kind of renewal ritual in which the women built a big fire while the men sang. If, while they were singing, they could hear the "Mother Spirit" sing, that was a sign the world was not coming to an end that year. This may have been connected with the ceremony of thanksgiving for the first fruits of the earth or the Green Corn Ceremony which was accompanied by a general amnesty for all crimes except murder. Another practice, possibly borrowed from the Iroquois, was the use of false faces. Among the Iroquois these distorted masks were cut from living trees and the ritual was conducted by a False Face Society in charge of social control. But little is known of the Shawnee practice. The masks were apparently not connected with a particular ceremony but used to frighten away evil spirits connected with disease and to purify the home. This practice did not appear in all Shawnee divisions, but David Jones, a missionary, encountered its use among the Ohio Shawnee. His frustration with the Shawnee is obvious in his account, and he characterizes their practices as barbaric.

The focus of Shawnee ritual was a pantheon of deities headed by the Great Spirit. Alford said the Great Spirit was addressed as "Grandmother." But Tenskwautawa, the Shawnee Prophet, indicates that the "Grandmother" was one of two subordinate deities under the Great Spirit and the one who had charge of the affairs of Indians. Her grandson, the other subordinate deity, was in charge of the whites.

The Shawnee also believed in "Motshee Monitoo," a bad spirit. His power was less than that of the Great Spirit, but to a limited degree he could punish and perplex men.

A belief in witches and the practice of witchcraft were also part of Shawnee life. Incurable illnesses were often blamed on witches, and persons suspected of practicing witchcraft were put to death. Incisions were made in the one who was bewitched so as to extract the combustible matter the witch had thrown into him. Such practices annoyed the Quakers at Wapakoneta, and on at least one occasion the missionaries protected a woman who was to be put to death as a witch.

Shawnee burial practices changed very little throughout their history. Certain practices changed over time and varied among the divisions, but in many details Shawnee mortuary practices remained the same. The body of the deceased was kept covered inside the dwelling for half a day after death; then it was prepared for burial by the blood kin of the dead person. The close kin chose a funeral leader and two or three corpse handlers who also served as gravediggers. None of the gravediggers could be related to the deceased nor be of the same name group. The funeral rites lasted four days and included purification rites, burial addresses, feasts, vigils, and condolence ceremonies.

Graves were dug about four feet deep and had an east-west orientation. The interior of the grave was sometimes lined with stone slabs, but most references indicate that wood and bark were used. The body was wrapped in a skin or covered with bark. Poles were laid across the top of the grave, bark was laid over the poles, and the earth taken from the grave was piled over the bark covering. A grave house made of logs or bark was erected over the graves. No cemeteries existed prior to 1830; most graves were dug near the dwellings.

The movement of Tenskwautawa the Prophet was in some ways a reassertion of traditional religious practices; but the major focus of this so-called revitalization was more secular and was in large measure a personality cult with the Prophet's brother, Tecumseh, at the center. The personality of Tecumseh was so powerful that even after his death his followers

Tenskwautawa, the Prophet
Painted by Charles Bird King
From Thomas L. McKenney and James Hall, *History of the
Indian Tribes of North America* (Philadelphia, 1842)

talked of his "second coming," when strife, wars, and contentions among Indian tribes would cease. This movement, which was most active from 1795 to 1811, was as much a reaction against white culture as it was a revitalization of traditional culture. Its pan-Indian flavor was certainly not in keeping with tradition, and actually attracted few Shawnee.

Tenskwautawa was older than Tecumseh but was not as impressive physically as his brother. While Tecumseh was strikingly tall, Tenskwautawa was of average height and a blind (or perhaps wandering) eye gave him a rather fierce look. He was, however, a very bright, perceptive, and commanding figure and was responsible for much of the ideological basis that attracted the disaffected to Tecumseh and his movement. He credited the Great Spirit for his insights regarding a return to the Indian way of life. The prohibition of European domesticates such as hogs, cattle, and sheep, and of wheaten bread, was a part of his nativistic preachings. Tenskwautawa told his followers that the buffalo and deer were created for their food and that Indians must wear the skins of these animals for clothing and make their bread of Indian corn. His harshest criticism was leveled at alcoholic beverages that weakened the Indian and gave the white man a means of taking advantage of him. Unfortunately much of his credence was lost at the disastrous battle of Tippecanoe in November of 1811. With Tecumseh in the South attempting to recruit the Choctaw and Creek to his cause, the Prophet, who did not have the military mind of his brother, miscalculated the strength of Governor Harrison's force and led his followers to defeat. The assurances that the Great Spirit would protect them from the American's bullets proved to be wrong. Tenskwautawa survived the War of 1812 but gave up his struggle. He eventually returned to Ohio and after migrating to Missouri with his village around 1825 he died there in 1834.

Shawnee folklore, music, and dance served both as amusement and as a part of the ceremonial activities. This expressive aspect of their culture was important to them and was retained even after their removal to Oklahoma.

The Shawnee myth of origin, like that of most peoples,

places them as the first of the Great Spirit's creations. It tells of their being transported over a large body of water from some unknown place and located on an island as the first people to inhabit the earth. The Shawnee folklore is flexible enough to incorporate new circumstances as they arise. One tale, as related by a local chief at Fort Wayne in 1803, tells of the Master of Life first making the Shawnee from his brain and all other red people became the descendants of the Shawnee. The French and English were then created from the Master's breast, the Dutch from his feet, and the long-knives (as the Virginians were called) from his hands. (The reason for separating the Virginians from the English is not stated.) All these inferior races were made white and placed beyond the "stinking lake."

Tales of the origin of the various divisions also exist. The Piqua, whose name means "a man coming out of the ashes," tell of an ancient fire that after burning out yielded a great puffing and blowing from which a man rose from the ashes. Mequachake signifies the perfect man of the Great Spirit's creation, and this is one reason for believing that the division was responsible for the priesthood.

Other tales are interesting in their simplicity. Rather than elaborate justifications or rationalizations of tribal events, the reasons are usually told in the form of some petty incident. The split between the Shawnee and Kickapoo and between the Shawnee and the Sauk and Fox has been mentioned as a result of a quarrel over some roasted bear paws. Similarly a break in an alliance between the Shawnee and Delaware in Pennsylvania is related in a tale about a fight over the possession of a grasshopper.

Shawnee music was more likely than their folklore to change and to incorporate elements borrowed from other tribes. The Cherokee and Creek had particularly great influence on Shawnee music and dance. Most songs were sung as an accompaniment to a wide variety of social and ceremonial dances. The singing was largely a male activity and was comprised of steady rhythmic chanting at various tempos depending on the nature of the dance. Many of the dances are couples' dances, but they begin with the men dancing in a circle and the women gradually entering, choosing a partner as they do so. The women's dance and the war dance are restricted to women and men respectively. The war dance includes a series of solo performances with each dancer recounting his own exploits in song. Songs and dances are accompanied by skin drums, gourd rattles, or both, depending on the dance. There are accounts of the use of reed flutes among the Shawnee, but apparently these were not used for the group songs and dances.

6

CONSERVATISM, DEPENDENCY, AND MIGRATION

NEXT TO MIGRATION, nothing about the Shawnee is so obvious as their conservatism. The reasons for this conservatism are not entirely clear. The historian Clark Wissler argued that the Shawnee never stayed in intimate contact with other tribal groups over sufficiently long periods of time for much diffusion to have taken place between them and their neighbors. Erminie Voegelin extends this, saying that they had contact with such a variety of cultures that they became aloof to all of them. Perhaps their extensive contacts with other Indian groups and with Europeans did help to stabilize native customs. But aloof they were not, for they freely borrowed material items such as guns, metal cookware, and clothing from the Europeans. The variety of their music indicates that the Shawnee borrowed and exchanged musical material wherever they went. Their conservatism was expressed in the very basic aspects of their subsistence. Thus, Shawnee conservatism was demonstrated not in their material trappings, but in the less observable but more important features of their society that were basic to their way of life.

Writing in 1908, folklorist Joab Spencer said of them: "The Shawnee cling to their old customs, seemingly more reluctant to abandon their ancient rites than any other civilized tribe. They regard their religious ceremonies of much importance." Their resistance to the influence of Christian missionaries was remarkable. The Moravians, who had much success with the Delaware, made few converts of the Shawnee. J. P. Klug, a Moravian missionary on the White River in Indiana, mentioned that "the few Shawnee who lived in that neighborhood were for the most part so carried away with their heathen teachers, that they did not want to hear anything [from the missionaries] of their [the heathen teachers'] foolish teaching." They also distrusted the Moravians' own religious teachings. Another missionary, David Jones, was driven out of Chillicothe in 1773 when he attempted to establish a mission among the Shawnee there. In an interesting account of a discussion between "the Count" (presumably the Moravian Count Zinzendorf) and Kakowatchekey, a Shawnee chief, the latter told the count that he believed in a God who had created the Indians as well as the Europeans, but, he said, the white men prayed with words, while the Shawnee prayed with their heart for which God respected the Indians; in fact, there was not much to the Europeans' prayer anyway—they were for the most part bad people.

Even when the Shawnee allowed missions to be established, they were reluctant to accept Christianity. The Friends succeeded in building a mission at Wapakoneta, Ohio, largely because the Quakers supported the Shawnee in their struggle against white encroachment and fraudulent land claims. For this the Shawnee accepted the mission and certain trappings of "civilization." But the Quakers had little success in converting them to Christianity.

In the latter part of the nineteenth century, Thomas Wildcat Alford, one of the first Shawnee educated in white schools, reflected on the difficulties he experienced. The people of his own village, including his parents, strongly opposed his going away to a "white man's school," for fear that he would adopt the white man's religion and ways. When he returned to establish a school, he was rejected and instead established a school among the Cherokee.

The Shawnee managed to withstand innovation in their religious ceremonies, and additions to their activities had little stability unless they fit into already established frames of reference. One aspect of their religion showing remarkable stability was their burial practice. While some southeastern tribes borrowed several customs from the Shawnee, few southeastern burial practices were adopted by the Shawnee.

The conservatism of Shawnee sociopolitical organization has already been indicated. The divisional and local autonomy seems to point to the retention of a political organization that had disappeared before historic times among the other Algonquian tribes. The Shawnee retained an emphasis on the village band, a type of organization reflective of an earlier structure more adaptive to a hunting way of life. Because of a lack of strong kin ties the Shawnee had more local population flexibility than normally found in agrarian societies. Villages could split and consolidate more easily when they did not have to worry about kinship-based residence rules.

Economic organization and subsistence also reflect the conservatism of the Shawnee. Farming, although practiced and ceremonially important, was not as highly esteemed as hunting and did not dominate the economic and social organization in the way that hunting did. Seldom were enough corn and other garden products raised to supply the Shawnee the year around. In the 1830s many Shawnee were still living as they had in the past, in groups that shifted seasonally from a summer village to a winter camp. Even after the Shawnee moved west of the Mississippi, hunting and trapping formed one of their major economic pursuits. Between 1835 and 1867 one group of Shawnee kept moving ahead of the frontier settlements into regions where trading posts were far apart and buckskins were available for moccasins, leggings, breech clouts, and hunting shirts. While the other eastern tribes settled to agricultural pursuits, the Shawnee maintained their small, family hunting organization.

Joab Spencer said: "Of all the Indian languages I ever heard, that of the Shawnees was most expressive, stately, eloquent and beautiful. They have a folk-lore of beauty and value." The retention of their language and folklore is remarkable, considering their dispersed locations and contacts with other languages and cultures. Even after extensive contact with the Creek Indians in Alabama, the Shawnee, unlike other tribes associated with the Creek confederacy, retained their own language and customs.

Given their penchant for conservatism, it is perhaps difficult to understand how the Shawnee were dependent upon other political or cultural groups for the maintenance of their cultural patterns. It would seem, at first glance, that the Shawnee could have been completely self-sufficient and would have undoubtedly preferred such a situation. But they, like all other American Indians, grew increasingly dependent upon European trade. There are some important aspects of this dependency which are relevant to Shawnee culture and conservatism.

A major aspect of this trade dependency related to the survival of the Shawnee or any other tribe. With the introduction of more efficient weapons and the adoption (particularly by the Iroquois) of European methods of warfare, wars of annihilation were possible. Lacking means of manufacture, the various tribes were dependent upon Europeans to supply these instruments, for without them the survival of the group was in serious jeopardy. The Shawnee were quick to see this and in fact were often in possession of weapons superior to those of their neighbors.

To procure these goods, pelts and skins were needed, and the latter could be more effectively obtained with guns and traps than with the traditional bow and arrow. This rationale fit neatly with the Shawnee emphasis on hunting but also created a cycle from which it was impossible to escape. Since hunting was the dominant and favored subsistence activity of the Shawnee, the increasing interest in skins, by other tribes as well as the Shawnee, tended to deplete sources of game and required a more efficient method of procuring game over greater distances. Thus to retain their village band hunting pattern the Shawnee relied even more on the guns and powder supplied by European traders.

Without a homeland to call their own the Shawnee were also dependent upon other tribes or political units to allow them to settle in a particular area and still keep their own conservative cultural patterns. This required permission to settle and hunt in a territory, and for this the Shawnee were often required to perform some service for the people upon whom they were dependent. As these requirements increased and began to threaten their way of life, the Shawnee moved to another locale where such pressures were felt to be less demanding. This was particularly true in regard to the relationships the Shawnee had with the Iroquois and the white governments. Other groups such as the Creek, Delaware, and Miami made few demands, except for mutual defense, and posed little threat to the Shawnee culture. Conservatism and dependency were key variables in the pattern of Shawnee migration. As motives, conservatism and dependency influenced the relations of the Shawnee with other political and social units and determined the favorability of various economic, political, and physical environments.

Shawnee migration from place to place was carried out in an orderly and efficient manner. The organization was determined in part by the size of the group, and the size was a function of the availability of food. When food was scarce, large groups split into small family groups while traveling, to make better use of food sources. A strict sexual division of labor was observed, and the line of march was a rank in single file with the women bringing up the rear. The men carried only their arms and bedroll and were responsible for supplying the meat along the journey. All the movable inventory that was transported from one location to another was carried by the women. Thus they carried little with them preferring instead to remake what they needed at their new site.

The pace of travel was slow by European standards, and the Shawnee were never in a hurry. Before breaking camp and beginning a day's march they would eat a hearty meal and mend clothing. Once started they seldom stopped until sunset, but they rarely traveled more than a few miles a day. If a family group killed a bear or other large animal they would stay in camp until it was consumed rather than carry it along. Often relocation involved a prolonged journey. The Shawnee might camp in one locality for weeks, or even months, waiting for floods to subside or taking advantage of favorable hunting conditions. Sometimes a crop of corn was planted and harvested before the journey was resumed.

Meat was the main sustenance while traveling, supplemented by corn flour eaten raw or used as a thickening for stew. Little effort was made to provide for other biological needs. Unless the camp stayed in one locale for a while, no shelters were built. The one exception was the construction of sweat houses in which the travelers soothed their tired muscles.

Although most Shawnee villages were along navigable streams, most of the travel was overland by foot. Wagons or travois were not used, and horses were not employed until relatively late. Rivers were crossed by wading, even in the winter. If the river was too deep to ford, the Shawnee would build rafts of logs tied together with vines or bark. Narrow streams might be crossed by felling a tree and walking across the trunk.

The Shawnee used the many paths that honeycombed the Eastern Woodlands. The complex network of trails and paths was remarkable in its adaptability to changing seasons and conditions of travel. Most Indian paths managed to keep nearly a direct course. The principles of trail locations were that the paths be dry, level, and direct. But the basic necessities of water, food, and clothing led the Indians to springs, salt licks, and other places where these could be obtained. On level terrain, animal trails often provided the most direct route to locations best supplying man's necessities. In the mountains or hills, trails often led along the higher ground and ridges. These ridge paths were more level than the mountain spines, were above the floodplain, and were well drained. Hilltops were windswept of snow in the winter and of brush and leaves in the summer. River trails were not extensively used by the Shawnee. The winding rivers were seldom a direct route; and large rivers, such as the Ohio, had steep slopes, cut by deep ravines, making travel along them impossible.

Storms or high water often made the narrow paths impassable, and for that reason a trail from one point to another usually had several paths. The path to be taken depended on the season, conditions, and the reasons for travel. After a storm, trails were made difficult by fallen trees and branches that were easier to go around than move and a path would adjust accordingly. Since the only routes in the western wilderness were these unmarked trails, the Cumberland region and the Ohio Valley remained free of white settlers for a long time. Wagons had to stop at the mountains, and the uncharted rivers were hazardous.

7

RELATIONS WITH OTHER INDIANS

THE EXTENSIVE migration of the various Shawnee divisions and bands brought them into contact with a large number of other Indian groups. Some of these encounters were brief and relatively insignificant, but others were extensive and played an important role in influencing the Shawnee. Unfortunately, except for a few references in the speeches of Shawnee chiefs, one must rely for information about these encounters on the accounts left by European observers. Many important intertribal ties were never recorded or observed, and those that were recorded are often sketchily described. Intertribal wars are better documented than peaceful relations and economic arrangements. In the following discussion on Shawnee relations with other tribes, some conclusions have had to be inferred rather than documented.

Two things should be observed in Shawnee migration into territories already occupied by indigenous tribal groups. One is the use of the migrating Shawnee by other political units, both white and Indian, as buffers against troublesome enemies. The other is the reaction of other tribes to Shawnee occupancy of their territory.

The Shawnee role as a buffer against troublesome natives is a recurrent one. They had early gained a reputation, perhaps of necessity, as fierce warriors. It has been suggested that they were invited to the Savannah River by the Cherokee for protection from the Catawba. There is no doubt that they were used in the same fashion by South Carolina whites against the Westo. In fact, Shawnee relationships with the Delaware, Conestoga, Miami, and even the Creek were each predicated on mutual defense against common enemies. As the Shawnee moved west of the Mississippi River they were used by the Spanish as a check against the troublesome Osage. The Shawnee who settled in Texas were used by the republic against the Wichita. In exchange for a place to settle, the Shawnee had become wandering mercenaries.

It is this role as mercenaries which determined the reactions of other tribes to Shawnee occupancy of territory claimed by these other tribes. Where they served as buffers and allies of locally indigenous Indian groups the Shawnee were welcomed. As allies of the Creek, Delaware, Miami, and Wyandot the Shawnee were granted land on which to establish their villages. But where they protected whites against other Indians, intertribal relations were generally hostile. Shawnee relations with the Iroquois, Osage, and Wichita as allies of the French, Spanish, and Texans, respectively, were of a hostile nature.

In the South the Shawnee had significant contacts with the Cherokee, Chickasaw, Creek, and Catawba. The Cherokee are an Iroquoian tribe which in the mid-seventeenth century occupied the mountainous region of the western Carolinas, eastern Tennessee, northeastern Alabama, and the adjacent area of northwestern Georgia. This location placed them directly between the Shawnee settlements in the Cumberland region and those in South Carolina. The most direct route for the Shawnee moving between the Cumberland River and South Carolina, and later between Pennsylvania and the Creek country, passed through Cherokee territory. Therefore contact between the Shawnee and Cherokee was inevitable.

It has even been suggested that the Cherokee and the Shawnee lived together in the same villages south of the Ohio

PAYTAKOOTHA, Flying Clouds
Shawnee signer of Treaty of Greenville, 1795
Painted by Charles Bird King
From Thomas L. McKenney and James Hall, *History of the Indian Tribes of North America* (Philadelphia, 1842)

River in prehistoric times. Although archaeological evidence cannot confirm this, relations between these tribes undoubtedly began before Europeans ever set foot in this region.

Since Shawnee locations on the Cumberland and at the headwaters of the Carolina rivers were on land claimed by the Cherokee, it can be assumed that the Shawnee had permission, or at least were allowed, to locate at these places. Shawnee settlements on the Savannah River may have been made at the invitation of the Cherokee, who desired to have their frontier protected against the Catawba. Yet most of the reports of political relations between the Cherokee and Shawnee before the American Revolution describe hostile encounters. In 1693 some of the Carolina Shawnee were raiding Cherokee villages for slaves. But most of the hostilities occurred during the French and Indian War, when Virginia employed the Cherokee to help resist Shawnee attacks on her frontier. Relations must have been mutually beneficial much of the time. Besides protecting the Cherokee's eastern frontier against the Catawba, the Shawnee also served as messengers between the Cherokee and Creek, who were often at war with each other. It was therefore useful for the Cherokee to maintain friendly relations with the Shawnee. The advantages of such a position for the Shawnee are obvious. Communications and travel could have been made difficult by a hostile Cherokee nation.

Shawnee settlements on the Cumberland River were also in close proximity to the Chickasaw, a Muskogean tribe located along the Mississippi River in the western part of the present states of Tennessee and Mississippi. The Chickasaw were often at odds with the Shawnee. Around 1700 the two tribes allied against the Tamaroa, an Illinois tribe, but this alliance was short-lived. In 1715 the Chickasaw and Cherokee united to drive the remaining Shawnee from the Cumberland Valley.

The Chickasaw were being courted by the French at this time, and it has been suggested that the war was a result of Chickasaw efforts to bring the Shawnee more closely under French influence. But it is doubtful that pressure for establishment of French ties would have occasioned sufficient grounds for a Shawnee confrontation with the Chickasaw; Shawnee bands had themselves established ties with the French more than two decades earlier in Illinois. But if this attempt at imposing French influence included the Chickasaw as middlemen, the Shawnee resistance is understandable. Such a situation would have placed the Shawnee in a subordinate role.

The next time we hear of Shawnee-Chickasaw relations is in 1756, when Peter Chartier and a band of Shawnee attempted to establish a village along the Tennessee River but were driven north by the Chickasaw. About this same time, according to Shawnee tradition, the French and Shawnee were allied in a war against the Chickasaw in which the latter were nearly annihilated.

The Shawnee and the Siouan-speaking Catawba, situated in South Carolina, were engaged in almost constant warfare. This fighting may have begun as early as 1670 when the Catawba are believed to have lived farther west, perhaps as far as the Kentucky River. But the continued hostilities were perpetuated largely by the Carolina traders and government.

Because of the constant wars many captives were taken, and the Indians found a ready market for them among the Charles Town slave dealers. Hostilities were originally aimed at the Spanish Indians from Florida, but the insatiable demand for slaves soon meant that the Indians who were allied with Carolina turned against each other. This situation was not discouraged and in fact was probably desired by the South Carolina authorities. Armed tribes, even allies, so close to the white settlements could be troublesome. If they could be worn down by intertribal warfare they would be less of a threat. To accomplish this the Carolina government supported the weaker tribes against the stronger ones. Just as the Shawnee had been given encouragement and support to make war on the Westo, the Catawba were later supported in order to keep the Shawnee in check.

The numerous raids by the Catawba caused many Shawnee

to leave South Carolina for Pennsylvania. Hostilities between the two tribes did not cease, however, as the Catawba continued to send war parties to Ohio and Pennsylvania while the Shawnee returned to raid the Catawba until at least 1762.

An understanding of the Shawnee relationship with the Creek is most important to an explanation of the Shawnee attraction to the Alabama region. These relations may not always have been pleasant, but no other region east of the Missouri River was occupied by a band of Shawnee in historic times as long as Alabama. There is evidence that some Shawnee bands lived with the Creek from at least 1685 to 1814. Besides hunting on the same land with the Creek, the Shawnee were permitted to settle in their territory for over a century.

The Shawnee who settled in Alabama were accepted as a part of the Creek confederacy and their towns were listed by the southern superintendent of Indians with the Creek villages. The Shawnee supported the Creek in their wars, and as late as 1814 they were allied against Andrew Jackson in the Creek War. The Creek made few demands other than military support from the Shawnee. Although forming a part of the Creek confederacy, Shawnee villages were self-governing and retained their own language and cultural patterns. Thus the Creek country offered the Shawnee an area in which they could maintain their conservative cultural patterns yet be both economically and militarily useful to the Creek.

In the Northeast the Conestoga, Delaware, and Iroquois were very influential in Shawnee history. When the Shawnee arrived in Pennsylvania in the late seventeenth century, the land along the lower Susquehanna River was the home of the Conestoga Indians. The Conestoga were Iroquoian speakers, variously known as Andaste by the French, Minquas by the Dutch, and Conestoga or Susquehanna by the English. Beginning in 1697 the Conestoga allowed bands of Shawnee from the Cumberland and Carolina regions to settle near them on the Susquehanna River.

Friendly relations between the Conestoga and Shawnee had

begun as early as 1663 when the Shawnee had been allies of the Conestoga in a conflict with the Iroquois Confederacy. These relations remained friendly until 1728 when two Conestoga Indians were murdered by some Shawnee. The murderers were protected by Peter Chartier and made their escape, a circumstance which caused the Conestoga to threaten war against the Shawnee. It was about this time that the Shawnee began to move west.

A close and lasting friendship existed between the Shawnee and the Algonquian-speaking Delaware Indians. The Walam Olum, the oral tradition of the Delaware, suggests that ties between these two tribes had existed for several decades before their joint occupation of the Delaware River Valley in the 1690s. This friendship continued as the Shawnee and Delaware moved west into Ohio and Missouri.

Shawnee migration from Illinois to Pennsylvania in the 1690s occurred as a result of an invitation from Matasit, a Delaware sachem, who had visited the Shawnee at Fort Saint Louis on the Illinois River. The Delaware offered the Shawnee land on which to settle and build their villages. When the Delaware were driven from their homes by the Pennsylvanians in 1742, the Shawnee, who had left earlier, returned the favor by inviting them to the Wyoming Valley along the Susquehanna. Later years found the Shawnee and Delaware living side by side in the Muskingum Valley of Ohio and near Cape Girardeau, Missouri.

Although the Shawnee called the Delaware "grandfather," there is no indication that this implied a dominant role for the Delaware in intertribal relationships. Some animosities existed between the Delaware and Shawnee but their relations were for the most part characterized by mutual respect and need.

The Iroquois occupied only a small portion of Pennsylvania and most of New York but laid claim to a far larger area by virtue of conquest. They had a long history of encounters with the Shawnee from Pennsylvania as far west as the Mississippi River.

Economic relations with the Iroquois were inevitable. Their claim to all land in Pennsylvania resulted in the development of relationships in which all other tribes were recognized as satellites, required to give their allegiance as subjects to the overall confederacy as a condition for occupying Pennsylvania territory. The Iroquois had served as middlemen to the Indians of the Ohio Valley for the British and Dutch traders from the 1650s. The Indians in Pennsylvania, however, traded directly with the British traders until William Penn's death. After his death in 1717, the Pennsylvania colonial government recognized all Iroquois claims, and the satellite tribes were expected to acknowledge the leadership of the League of the Iroquois in major matters of trade, war, and diplomacy.

Although the Shawnee were friendly with the Iroquoian-speaking Mingo in Ohio, Shawnee relations with most of the Iroquois had never been good. There is reliable evidence that the Iroquois had driven the Shawnee from the Ohio Valley in the mid-seventeenth century and had carried this war as far west as Illinois, where they made attacks against the Shawnee in 1684. It must have been with some apprehension that the Shawnee settled in Pennsylvania on the border of this powerful confederacy. For a time the seemingly benevolent policies of William Penn made conditions in the colony tolerable for the Shawnee. By 1727, however, the Iroquois had solidified their hold over the Pennsylvania tribes and maintained agents who acted as overlords in the vicinity of Delaware and Shawnee villages. When Conrad Weiser took control of Pennsylvania Indian policy in the 1730s, the Shawnee and Delaware were already moving west. An adopted Iroquois, Weiser had little regard for the Delaware and Shawnee, and he created a situation that the Shawnee could not tolerate.

Although Shawnee relations with the other tribes in the upper Ohio Valley must have been frequent and important, little is known about their nature except for what is revealed by an occasional reference to the Western Confederacy, which included the Miami, Delaware, Wyandot, and Shawnee. Some mention has been made of the Miami and Wyandot, but even this is taken largely from indirect sources. The Miami, an Algonquian tribe closely related linguistically to the Shawnee, were situated in what is today Indiana and western Ohio. The Wyandot were the remnant of the Huron, who had been defeated by the Iroquois confederacy. Still powerful warriors, they claimed the Ohio Valley and the lake region.

It was at the invitation of the Miami that the Shawnee ventured into Ohio around 1684, perhaps to help the Miami defend themselves against attacks from the Iroquois. Shawnee bands were again welcomed by the Miami in the mid-eighteenth century. Drawn perhaps by the French trade, the Miami were moving west into Indiana, and the Shawnee settled on land they vacated. Because of Wyandot claims to this region, it was only with their consent and by their permission that the Shawnee and Miami occupied lands north of the Ohio River.

The Miami helped the Shawnee to resist the white man's advance into the Ohio Valley. Like the Miami, the Wyandot were important allies of the Shawnee in the wars against the settlers and were one of the largest groups in Tecumseh's army during the War of 1812. Tenskwautawa said the Wyandot tribe was one of those with which the Shawnee never had a war.

Other tribes in the Old Northwest were also important to the Shawnee. The Illinois, Kickapoo, and Sauk and Fox, Central Algonquian speakers, are mentioned by Tenskwautawa as close allies of the Shawnee. But records regarding specific Shawnee relations with these tribes are sparse.

Shawnee relations with other Indian groups were reflective of patterns in Shawnee society. Their dependency and conservatism served as guidelines in defining their reaction to the peoples with whom they came in contact. It is therefore not surprising that their ties with the Creek, Cherokee, and Delaware were long lasting. The reciprocating relationship developed with these tribes was combined with a mutual respect for tribal autonomy. The hostile nature of the Shawnee's relationship to the Chickasaw, Catawba, and Iroquois can be understood in the same manner. Contacts with these groups were not established on the basis of mutual need, and neither the Chickasaw nor the Iroquois respected the autonomy and independence of the Shawnee. These patterns undoubtedly determined the relationships with other tribes as well, even where contacts were brief.

8

RELATIONS WITH WHITES

SHAWNEE RELATIONS with whites were complex, based in part on their resistance to European culture, in part on economic realities, and in part on the various Indian policies of the colonies and later the United States.

It is somewhat misleading to generalize about colonial Indian policy, for the lack of a uniform, just system for managing Indian affairs characterized the colonial period. So lax was the central control of Indian affairs that policy was actually made in many instances by those who had contact with the Indians. Nevertheless, certain attitudes prevailed which determined the nature of Indian-white relations. Since in some ways these attitudes differed from one colonial power to another, policies differed as well.

Economic activities include both trade and land relations. For the Shawnee, trade was one of the few avenues of contact with whites and by far the most extensive. Shawnee survival depended on trade goods, particularly firearms. But beyond this, the Shawnee early gave up material crafts as goods of European manufacture became readily available. No tribe could exist without the support of the white nations; they would not live as their ancestors had before the arrival of the Europeans.

The whites were aware of this Indian dependency and used

trade with the natives as the foundation for Indian alliances. Trade was the first principle of the whole system of Indian politics. Even after the fur trade ceased to be economically important to most British colonists, many saw it as being the most effective means of countering Indian alliances with the French, for whom furs were the major economic export.

Occupation of land and treaties regarding this matter were also important considerations and often outweighed trade in influencing Shawnee-white relations. Without a homeland, the Shawnee were sensitive to negotiations and treaties that affected their settlement and use of land. White settlement of land occupied and used by the Shawnee also threatened their conservative way of life.

A discussion of Shawnee political relations with the whites necessarily bears upon military affairs. Apart from trade relations and land negotiations, both economic in nature, most of the other formal contacts the Shawnee established with the white governments involved military alliances, treaties of neutrality, or wars. Although the wars are significant to Shawnee history, they are less important than the reasons for Shawnee involvement or, in many cases, lack of involvement. The focus will therefore not be on the hostilities but on the economic and cultural factors leading to alliances, neutrality, or war.

In *The Jesuits in North America*, historian Francis Parkman compared the French Indian policy with that of the Spanish and British, noting that the Spanish crushed the Indian, the English scorned and neglected him, but the French embraced and cherished him. Parkman's pro-French sentiments result in a comparison that is somewhat overdrawn, but, in fact, the French did have better relations with the Indians than did the other colonial powers. There are several reasons why this was so.

Fur trade was the life of Canada, and trading ties with the Indians were important to the French. The geography of Canada, with the Saint Lawrence River linked to the chain of Great Lakes, aided the establishment of Indian ties by opening the interior to French penetration. Eager to conciliate the

Indians, the French learned their language, customs, and prejudices, and showed a readiness to adopt their ways. Unlike the British, French traders mingled and intermarried with the Indians.

Martin Chartier provides an example both of the advantages the French had in dealing with the Indians and of the problems they experienced with their traders. One major difficulty was the independence and the lack of loyalty of the French traders. Often their reason for being in the New World in the first place was that they were not wanted in France. Therefore an allegiance to France was not one of their virtues. Chartier appeared on a list of deserters from La Salle's party in 1680. By 1689 he had married a Shawnee woman and was living with the Indians along the Cumberland River near present-day Nashville. He was with this group when they moved to Pennsylvania and established a village near the town of Conestoga. He did not give up his trading, however, and built a trading post there and later at Dekuneagah, on the Susquehanna River. But he was independent and, although French, probably obtained his supplies from British merchants. Martin died at Dekuneagah in 1718 but left a son, Peter, who continued to live with the Shawnee as they moved into western Pennsylvania and Ohio. Although they were certainly not the leaders of their respective villages, their presence was noted by Europeans and the towns were often identified as "Chartier's Town" or "Chartier's Band."

Peter Chartier continued to serve as a trader and had a post on the Allegheny River from 1735 to 1745. But after plundering some Pennsylvania traders of their furs, he fled his village and joined another group of Shawnee on the Scioto River in Ohio. From there he may have moved to Eskippakithiki in Clark County, Kentucky. He is said to have stayed two years there before he moved again to Alabama. In 1755 he was on the Tennessee River, but trouble with the Chickasaw drove him back to the Ohio at the present site of Shawneetown, Illinois. Nothing more is recorded of his whereabouts and perhaps he died there. Some of the Shawnee situated there eventually returned to Ohio. Others moved to Missouri, but no mention is made of Chartier. It is not known if he married or had any children, but it was ties such as those he and his father established with the Shawnee that gave the French an advantage in the Indian trade.

French officials, as opposed to French traders, displayed power which, though sometimes abused, was designed to garner respect. When diplomacy failed, the French often resorted to force. Behind all this was a strong centralization of control and demand for allegiance to the crown. French policy, though cumbersome at times, was consistent and coordinated.

Probably as important in maintaining good relations as any other fact was the French failure to attract settlers to Canada. The few white men who resided there took up little land; there was no wholesale takeover of Indian territory. Large tracts were claimed by the French for the crown; but, since the Indians were included as subjects and no French settlers desired the land, the Indians remained free to pursue their own interests.

The earliest record of trade which specifically mentions the Shawnee is the account of La Potherie, a French trader who in 1677 traded with a Shawnee residing with the Potawatomi. The Shawnee were probably receiving trade goods before this date from Indian middlemen employed by European trading companies. In the early seventeenth century, Indians of the Lower Ohio Valley were obtaining items of European manufacture through the Huron Indians. The Iroquois soon defeated the Huron and took over this role as middlemen. To counteract the influence of the Iroquois, who soon were in league with the British, the French undertook to establish forts along the Ohio River. By 1682 La Salle succeeded in building a post at Starved Rock on the Illinois River. The Shawnee, who by this time were residing in the Cumberland region, preferred to deal with the French directly rather than to obtain British goods through the Iroquois.

The Shawnee in South Carolina had established trading ties with the British. Those who moved to Alabama in 1715 continued relations with the Carolina traders until the 1750s, but they were also being courted by the French. Even before 1700 Shawnee from as far east as South Carolina were trading with the French at New Orleans. In 1714 the French built a store among the Shawnee near present-day Nashville. When Vaudreuil was governor of Louisiana in the mid-eighteenth century, the Alabama Shawnee were trading exclusively with the French.

Until 1730 the French trader was not a serious rival for Shawnee trade in western Pennsylvania and the upper Ohio Valley. The English had many advantages, including a monopoly on rum and strouds, lower manufacturing costs on other articles, and a better flow of goods. The French, who had to import their goods through Montreal, were dependent on the Saint Lawrence River, which was closed by the northern ice for nine months out of the year.

Though the quality and prices of French goods were not competitive with those of British offerings, there were features of French policy attractive to the Shawnee. The French did not treat the Indians as inferiors. There was little attempt to Europeanize the Indians. The French had better success in prohibiting abuses in the sale of alcohol. In general the French traders treated the natives more fairly than their British rivals, who often practiced violence, as well as deception and fraud.

As early as 1728 Shawnee leaders were invited to Montreal, where they were well received and lavished with presents. French diplomats were sent to Shawnee villages on the Ohio with blacksmiths to repair guns, hoes, and hatchets without pay. The Shawnee did not refuse these advances, but neither did they wish to give up their trade with the British. Trade was important to the Shawnee, and alignment with the French would cut them off from important sources of goods.

The French apparently had no set policy of extinguishing Indian titles to land. They merely took possession without any pretense of purchase and claimed the domain for the king. This was done peaceably if possible, with force if necessary. Because of their small numbers, however, the French were not a threat to the natives' land, particularly in the Ohio Valley.

KISHKALWA
A Shawnee chief who took part in the battle of Point Pleasant, 1774
Painted by Charles Bird King. From Thomas L. McKenney and James Hall,
History of the Indian Tribes of North America (Philadelphia, 1842)

In addition, the French policy, unlike the British, was to accept the Indian as one of their own. Even on land claimed by the king, as the Ohio Valley was, the Indians were not disturbed and were allowed to live where they were without changing their culture.

The British contention that the Shawnee were French Indians, that is, within the French political sphere, is not borne out by historical evidence. Until 1754 there was no significant Shawnee military support of the French. Even the alliance in the French and Indian War was based in part on the lack of British military support for the Shawnee against the bullying tactics of the French in the Ohio Valley.

The French had courted the Shawnee for a long time prior to their military alliance during the French and Indian War. When economic enticement failed, the French threatened the Shawnee with military reprisals. Alone the Shawnee could not stand against the French and their Indian allies. Pennsylvania refused to garrison its western border to protect the Indians from the French. Efforts by Virginia to do so became weakened by speculators from the Ohio Company, which had been granted the land north of the Ohio River. These speculators were more interested in surveying land than in protecting their sources for Indian trade. By 1754 the French alternative was more attractive to the Shawnee than having British settlements continually push them from their land with no compensation whatsoever. Only when confronted with having to choose between these opposing pressures did the Shawnee agree to form a military alliance with France.

Before the French and Indian War the various British colonies were largely responsible for their own relations with the Indian tribes. Although there was no uniform policy, certain basic features became fixed in all the colonies. The colonists who helped mold Indian policy held strongly racist attitudes, considering the Indians a separate order, distinguished by their culture, savagery, and color. Unlike the French and Spanish, the British rarely intermarried with the Indians, and it was soon apparent that the two groups were not to live in peace easily.

To maintain peace, the British colonies developed a body of restrictions designed to prevent or regulate contact between the whites and the Indians. The result was that the Indians were pushed back and replaced on the land by whites. As early as 1653 the English began assigning some tribesmen to reservations. This became a basis for conflict, and the two groups viewed each other with suspicion and hostility.

Trade became the predominant point of contact between the British and Indians for two reasons. Indian trade was important economically for some colonies inasmuch as furs became their major export. But for the British, Indian trade was even more important politically. Peace and the very existence of the colonies depended on Indian attachment to the English. Although presents were used to ensure the allegiance of the tribes, trade was of still greater significance in effecting the desired relationship.

But the lack of a centralized and uniform trade policy resulted in political failure. The British colonies competed for Indian favor, not only with other European nations but with each other, and this situation resulted in much abuse. Restrictions on trade in such items as liquor or firearms differed from colony to colony. Enforcement of such regulations as existed was nearly impossible against the unscrupulous trader, who was the rule rather than the exception. This chaotic situation, coupled with fraudulent land purchase, contributed greatly to the French and Indian alliance in the war that began in 1754. British attempts to rectify the situation by centralizing authority and establishing a uniform system of Indian management had to be abandoned. The independence of the provincial governments and their hatred of the Indians precluded effective cooperation among the colonies.

Shawnee relations with the British probably began in the mid-seventeenth century with the Iroquois as middlemen in a trading network. But it was in South Carolina that the Shawnee first established direct ties with the British. The first active Shawnee-white military alliance was with South Carolina, when they acted as a buffer for the colony, particularly against the pro-Spanish Indians. But the most important tie for the colony was the trade relationship that was established. Unable to find a suitable staple crop to grow, the Carolinians turned to the fur trade in search of wealth. Although the back country was not as accessible to the Carolinians as it was to the traders of Florida and Louisiana, the English sold better quality goods at cheaper prices than either the Spanish or French.

By 1674 extensive trade with the Creeks had been built by Carolina traders. South Carolina desired to control the Indian trade to the Mississippi, and in 1682 British trade included the Shawnee. Even a partial list of the goods provided by the Carolina traders indicates how dependent the material culture of the Indians had become. The inventory included guns, bullets, powder, knives, hoes, blankets, shirts, kettles, and rum.

Originally the Indian trade was controlled by the proprietors of the colony, but by 1710 it was in the hands of Charles Town merchants. Traders, either on their own or in the employ of these merchants, were seldom scrupulous in their methods of obtaining slaves and skins, and their abuses, which became notorious, included price gouging, overextension of credit (which indebted the Indian to a particular trader, who then sold at inflated prices), watering down the rum, and enslavement of free Indians.

In spite of the abuses, the Indian trade expanded. But rice was becoming a profitable crop, and farmers who had no interest in the fur trade began to push inland. With this, political relations between the Shawnee and the colonists deteriorated, and by 1715 the Shawnee remaining in South Carolina joined in an open revolt against the British colony, a conflict known as the Yamasee War.

Shawnee relations with William Penn were always cordial. He was fair in trading with the Indians and his land policy was geared to placate all parties, even when claims conflicted. A broad belt of purchased land had always been kept between the frontier settlers and the Indians' eastern claims. Pennsylvania was not strongly oriented to the fur trade, but some such relations were established with the Indians residing within the colonial boundaries. This trade was carefully controlled by William Penn, who had to approve the transactions and who prohibited the use of alcohol for trading purposes. Penn also insisted that goods traded to the Indians be of good quality.

Trade may not have been the major factor attracting the Shawnee to Pennsylvania, but surely it was an important consideration. The seeming benevolence and rigid trading standards of Penn made his colony more attractive than most. The quality and variety of goods obtainable from the British traders were important to the Shawnee. In exchange they bartered deer, elk, buffalo, and bear skins; beaver, raccoon, fox, cat, muskrat, mink, fisher, and other furs; food supplies; and sometimes personal services.

However, with the death of William Penn in 1717, relations between the Shawnee and the colony of Pennsylvania deteriorated. Even before Penn's death, troubles with British traders were of concern to the Shawnee. As in South Carolina, most of the problems lay less in formal policy than in the character of the men attracted to the Indian trade. This trade was carried on, with some few exceptions, by the vilest of residents and by convicts imported from Great Britain and Ireland. As early as 1701 the Shawnee complained of a trader who had brought them rum and much abused them when they drank it to excess. Although laws prohibiting the sale of liquor to the Indians still existed, the proprietary government after Penn's death could not, or found it profitable not to, enforce them. Rum brought good profits to the trader both as a sales item and as a means of weakening the Indians' bargaining power for other goods.

Other changes in trade relations followed the death of William Penn. The 1701 treaty between Pennsylvania and the Indians, including the Shawnee, had stipulated that the natives trade only with Pennsylvanians. But as a result of Queen Anne's War in 1710 the Iroquois acted as middlemen in the fur trade for the British in the Ohio Valley. With the appointment of Conrad Weiser as the head of the Indian service in the 1730s the dominance of the Iroquois was assured. The severe restrictions on the traders were lifted, and Pennsylvania became heavily involved in fur trading. To insure that furs would not go to competitors, traders were liberal with credit, which kept the Indians in debt and resulted in much abuse.

Trade was not the only area of concern between the Shawnee and the Pennsylvanians. The British were permanent settlers whose expanding population needed land—land that was occupied by the Indians. Where William Penn had been fair to all parties, his heirs were indifferent to the concerns of the Shawnee and Delaware and permitted settlers to occupy unpurchased land. Although the Shawnee had no real claim to land in Pennsylvania, they were much upset at this practice. When Pennsylvania recognized only Iroquois claims to the land drained by the Delaware River, the Shawnee felt betrayed and demanded reparations, a request that Pennsylvania ignored.

The unrestrained traffic in rum and Pennsylvania's new land policy drove a large number of Shawnee to the Ohio River in the 1730s. By moving west the Shawnee did not intend to cut off trading ties with the British. In the 1730s, however, the French began to woo the friendship of the western tribes and many Shawnee began to trade with them at Detroit.

The struggle between the French and British was escalating at this time. Although it was increasingly difficult, the Shawnee attempted to remain neutral in this colonial struggle. The English colonies eventually drove the Shawnee to their subsequent alliance with the French. By the Treaty of Lancaster in 1744 the Virginians purchased from the Iroquois the "lands to the setting sun." Taking this literally, the Virginians acted accordingly. Virginia's design on the Ohio country was formalized when land on the upper Ohio River was granted to the Ohio Company. The Ohio Indians who signed this treaty agreed to English settlement on the south and east of the Ohio River, but their interpretation of the treaty denied any English claim to lands west of the mountains. The Shawnee, however, were not a party to this treaty and did not feel obligated to abide by any part of it.

What the French could not gain through competition and presents they managed to achieve by threat and force. To keep the Shawnee from trading with the British, the French threatened them with retaliation if they continued to deal with Pennsylvania traders. Without protection the Shawnee were no longer able to retain their position of noninvolvement, and for the first time openly sided with the French against the British. From 1754 to 1763 the Shawnee made raid after raid on the British frontier settlements, particularly in western Virginia and Kentucky.

The British victory in the French and Indian War may have ended the political rivalry east of the Mississippi, but it did not end the competition for trade. From 1763 to 1775 Indian trade relations with the British were chaotic. The British fortified the frontier against French incursions and tried to require the Indians to trade at their forts. But the French from Louisiana crossed the Mississippi and traded directly with native villages. As a result, the stringent trade restrictions of the British were largely ignored, and by 1768 the forts were abandoned along with trade regulations.

George Croghan, a Pennsylvania trader, succeeded in establishing trading ties with the Shawnee, and so long as he maintained a trading post the Shawnee were frequent visitors. But as interest in land increased, the importance of the Indian trade lessened. The number and value of skins and furs purchased by the British decreased every year from 1763 to 1775. One last effort by the British to regulate trade and stem the abuses came in 1774 when the western areas were placed under the Quebec government. With the Quebec Act the Board of Trade hoped to provide the necessary regulation, but the attempt came too late.

Even after the French defeat, the Ohio Shawnee remained hostile to the British and were the last tribe to give up their prisoners. Many took an active part in Pontiac's rebellion and the siege of Detroit. As late as 1765 the Shawnee asked the governor of Louisiana for aid against the English who were taking Shawnee land.

The Proclamation Line of 1763, drawn down the Appalachian divide, was designed to keep white settlers from violating the rights of the Indians. Unfortunately the line was often violated. Where the Indians saw it as a fixed boundary, whites viewed it as only temporary. Shawnee suspicions of this attitude were borne out at Fort Stanwix in 1768. The British purchased from the Iroquois the vast tract of land lying between the Appalachian divide and the Ohio River as far west as the Tennessee River, including nearly all of Kentucky as well as lands to the northeast. The Iroquois claimed this territory by virtue of conquest, but the Shawnee recognized no such claim and refused to acknowledge the cession.

It was obvious that the Ohio Valley could not be settled without a war with the Shawnee. But the Pennsylvania merchants, including George Croghan, knew any frontier disturbance would injure their trade with the Indians. Besides, Croghan and several of his associates were interested in the Vandalia scheme, an attempt to colonize large portions of Pennsylvania and western Virginia (including the eastern half of what is now Kentucky), and did not wish to see Virginians occupy any of this country.

On the Virginia side Colonels George Washington and William Preston were leading proponents of the land claims of French and Indian War veterans, and they, with Dr. Thomas Walker, pushed for settlement of the Ohio Valley. In direct violation of instructions from the crown, surveyors and speculators from Virginia, including William Crawford, Thomas Bullitt, and James Harrod, were working in Kentucky from 1772 to 1774. Support forces accompanying these surveyors began to attack Shawnee hunting parties, and Lord Dunmore, governor of Virginia, authorized sending militia to protect the Virginians. All-out war resulted. This conflict, known as Lord Dunmore's War, involved nearly all of the Shawnee in the Ohio Valley and was one of the bloodiest wars in Shawnee history.

Pennsylvania traders protested that the Virginians were trying to destroy the trade. The Virginians countered with charges that Pennsylvania traders were buying goods stolen from the whites and encouraging the Shawnee to repel or kill the Virginia settlers. The war was really a territorial dispute between Pennsylvanians and Virginians, with the Shawnee serving as pawns in the struggle.

The fact that settlement west of the mountains was prohibited by the Proclamation of 1763 was academic by the time troops were sent. Perhaps it was because the land was granted illegally that the Virginians pursued an all-out war to defeat the Shawnee and make them give up the land. The Virginians picked up help when Sir William Johnson, the northern Indian superintendent, convinced the Shawnee's western allies to remain neutral. The war began in July of 1774 when one party of volunteers was ambushed by a group of Shawnee warriors, and the struggle escalated rapidly as Governor Dunmore sent some 1,500 militia from western Virginia. Under the command of Colonel Andrew Lewis, on October 6, the militia met a large force of Shawnee under the leadership of Chief Cornstalk at Point Pleasant, where the Great Kanawha River joins the Ohio. Heavy losses were experienced on both sides, but Cornstalk finally gave up and accepted defeat. In the Treaty of Camp Charlotte that followed, the Shawnee were forced to give up all rights to land south of the Ohio River.

For the Shawnee the Revolution was an extension of Lord Dunmore's War. Many of the revolutionaries were the same people against whom the Shawnee had fought in 1774. There is some indication that the Shawnee were at first divided over renewing the fight with these adversaries, but the murder of Chief Cornstalk in 1777 angered the Shawnee who originally had not joined the alliance, and they now took up arms.

Cornstalk, also known as Hokolesqua, was a hereditary chief of the Chillicothe division and thus nominally the chief of the entire Shawnee tribe. He did not particularly favor an all-out war with the whites again, but neither did he want to lose land in Kentucky to settlers. He emerged as a powerful and skillful war leader during skirmishes with the Virginians as the latter illegally claimed and settled land west of the Alleghenies. But Cornstalk was, like all Shawnee leaders, a capable orator as well. He knew the treaties and spoke from a position of what he perceived to be right and what he knew to be just. His speech at the Treaty of Charlotte struck out eloquently at the numerous wrongs suffered by the Shawnee at the hands of the Virginians and other European colonists.

In spite of his ability as a warrior, he did not want to put his people in a position he knew would only speed their doom. He was the whites' only hope for a peaceful relationship with the Shawnee on the frontier. After the Treaty of Charlotte he did his best to keep his people from joining in an alliance against the settlers in western Virginia. But in a peace mission to the fort at Point Pleasant to warn the whites of conditions on the frontier he was detained along with his son Elinipsico and sub-chief Red Hawk. During his detention two soldiers sent outside the fort to collect firewood were fired upon, and one was killed. In retaliation some of the soldiers killed the three captives. Despite the insistence of Patrick Henry, governor of Virginia, that the murderers be brought to justice, they were not; and the militia became involved in full-scale warfare with the Shawnee once again.

Even as the Revolution was being fought, speculators and settlers were pushing into what is now Kentucky. They were less concerned with the war than with acquiring land. Their new settlements were constantly threatened by attacks from the Shawnee, who still claimed Kentucky as their hunting territory. Because of these attacks a pronounced hatred of the Shawnee developed among these Kentucky settlers, and the war between the Kentucky militia and the Shawnee continued long after the close of the Revolution.

The Indian policy of the United States had the same basic focus as that of the British. The problems inherited from the British grew out of the fact that the Indians had been on the land when the white man arrived, and their presence was viewed as an obstacle to the westward advance of white settlers. The goal of American Indian policy was the peaceful advance of the frontier. To accomplish this the United States, like the British, attempted to keep order by restricting contacts between the whites and Indians. The laws enacted were thus restrictive and prohibitory, designed to provide a modicum of justice for the Indians, but also to open the way for American settlement. Unlike the British colonies, the United States developed a single unified policy rather than several independent ones, and there was for at least a century a general consistency in approach.

But the policy set forth in the laws was not necessarily an expression of the attitudes of frontier settlers. Their hostility toward the Indian and their disregard for the restrictive laws made it impossible for the government to carry out its policy. The goal of a peaceful advance broke down as the Indian-hating frontiersman disregarded Indian rights. The result was an advance filled with conflict and injustice to the Indians.

After the Revolution the fur trade of the Ohio Valley received special attention from the Continental Congress of the United States. An agent of Indian affairs on the Ohio was appointed and given responsibility for the direction and inspection of the trade. Congress also provided that two stores be opened, one on the Muskingum River and the other on the Scioto at Lower Shawnee Town. All who traded with the Indians had to be licensed by the governor of the territory of the United States north of the Ohio River.

In spite of congressional attention, trade relations were unsuccessful in the early years. Without goods for trade and gifts it was difficult to procure allies during the Revolution. Arguing that the people of the back country, who were violently prejudiced against the Indians, could not be expected to furnish such goods, the states refused to lend assistance. Aversion to furnishing supplies to the Indians was a barrier to amicable Indian relations long after the Revolution. The hatred of the Shawnee for the American settlers was no less strong, and this mutual hostility inevitably resulted in conflict.

In 1782 the Shawnee were joined by the Delaware, Wyandot, Miami, Ottawa, Chippewa, and Mingo in a confederacy to drive the settlers from Kentucky and Ohio. Their first confederated battles took place at Bryan Station and Blue Licks, Kentucky, in August of 1782. They were repulsed at Bryan Station, but when pursued to Blue Licks they defeated a militia led by Daniel Boone. In 1792, Henry Knox, secretary of war, claimed that the sole cause of the continuing war was the unprovoked aggression of the Shawnee and their confederated tribes. Certainly there are numerous accounts of Shawnee aggression against the Kentucky and Ohio settlers; but that these attacks were unprovoked is certainly not the case. Depredations against the Shawnee were numerous and cruel. Between 1779 and 1790 the Shawnee village of Chillicothe on the Little Miami River was attacked five times and completely destroyed on four of those occasions. Shawnee victims were often scalped by American soldiers; prisoners were subjected to torture and even burned at the stake.

The British were also involved in perpetuating these wars. They warned the Shawnee that to make peace with the United States would mean starvation, poverty, and removal from their land. The British offered bounties for settlers' scalps. One captive of the Shawnee observed warriors making scalps from the humps of buffalo and surmised that these were to be sold as human scalps to the British.

As the flood of settlers and troops into the Ohio Valley continued, it became increasingly difficult and costly for the Shawnee to resist the advance. The British, who had encouraged resistance, refused direct help. The final blow for the Shawnee came in 1794 when American troops led by General Anthony Wayne defeated the Shawnee at Fallen Timbers, Ohio. A few Shawnee later joined with Tecumseh and continued to resist until the War of 1812. But most of them reluctantly agreed to the Greenville treaty of 1795 and ceded all their land south of the Ohio River, together with most of present-day Ohio and southern Indiana to the United States.

In the Treaty of Greenville in 1795 Anthony Wayne promised the Ohio Valley Indians satisfactory trading conditions in the form of a new "factory" system, which amounted to no more than government-owned trading posts. The government did not intend to make a profit but did hope that its factories would be self-supporting. Such a post was established at Fort Wayne in 1802 to control the Ohio Valley trade, but it had a less than auspicious beginning. The kinds of goods suitable for the Indian trade were not sent to the store. Transportation of goods was slow, and often articles were embezzled on the way or arrived damaged. The necessary skills for trading with the Indians were rare in the United States. Although Fort Wayne had five licensed traders, all were Canadians. Private American traders and the British did all they could to undermine the new system; they were more successful than the agents at the factories, who had to operate according to government regulations.

After the initial problems were resolved, however, the Fort Wayne factory began to show signs of survival and even made a profit. Much of this success must be attributed to John Johnston, who served as the factor at Fort Wayne from 1804 to 1811. He gained the respect of the Indians through fair trading practices and a genuine concern for their welfare. At the Shawnee's request he served as their agent from 1812 until their removal in 1832. Another reason for the growing American success was the Indians' increasing dissatisfaction with the British. While the British encouraged the western Indians to rebel against the United States, they refused to give direct military support. In 1812 only a few Shawnee, led by Tecumseh, actually took up arms on the British side.

By that time the factories were offering a variety of trade goods at prices competitive with those offered by the British. In addition to the standard fare, such goods included spelling books, Bibles, corn mills, plowshares, garden seeds, and other items reflective of plans to "civilize" the natives. Where deer and beaver had been the major export of the British and French colonies, raccoon was by far the most abundant pelt traded at the Fort Wayne agency. Deer were still important, but beaver had become nearly extinct.

Trade was not the only economic concern the Americans had with the Indians. The land policy of the United States was based on the theory that all the land was held by the natives. It became necessary to adopt some procedure to extinguish Indian rights to such territory as the Americans desired. Until 1871 the tribes were recognized as independent nations, and land titles were extinguished only by formal treaties. Since tribes were in actuality not independent nations with well-defined boundaries and centralized leadership, no one individual had the authority to transfer, by sale, the soil on which his tribe lived. But to satisfy the fiction of the legal transfer, the Americans needed only to find or create a headman who claimed such authority. Though their land could be taken only through formal treaty, the Shawnee had neither the military power nor the will to resist. Many of the treaties with the Shawnee were obtained by threat or fraud, but by 1830 the Ohio Shawnee were confined to two small reservations in the northwestern corner of that state; two years later the Shawnee had ceded to the United States all their land east of the Missouri River.

Although the implementation of the factory system had improved capacity for trading with the Indians, this development had little to do with the Shawnee's decision to end their political and military struggle with the United States. The conflict had begun over land, not trade; and the end of the conflict was military victory, not a resolution of the problem. Since the land allotted them did not provide enough territory on which fur-bearing animals could be obtained, the Shawnee's capacity to trade decreased. Those located in the Ohio Valley became increasingly dependent upon annuities paid by the government for land ceded to the United States through the various treaties. Others chose to exchange their domain for land in Louisiana territory, west of the Mississippi River, an alternative more attractive to many who did not wish to live so close to American settlers. The latter arrangement merely postponed the inevitable, however, for by 1864 all Shawnee were living on reservations in Indian Territory, depending in large measure on annuity payments and what little they could produce by farming.

It is apparent from this summary that Shawnee-white political relations were dependent upon economic relations. Trade relations were very important both to the Shawnee and to the whites, but often for different reasons. The Shawnee were economically dependent upon trade for arms and other basic necessities. Though some of the colonies were dependent upon furs and skins as a major economic export, political ties became the most important reason for establishing trade with the Indians. Shawnee allegiance or at least neutrality was gained by both France and England because of trading ties. Even the abuses by British traders were not sufficient to alienate the Shawnee completely. Their dependence on British goods kept them from aligning against the British colonies until very late.

Land relations were the basic consideration in Shawnee political affairs. The continual white expansion into territory occupied or used by the Shawnee was the major cause for alienation. The Shawnee's dependency on trade postponed the political break, but the open hostilities against the whites were predominantly sparked by the westward expansion. This expansion was seen by the Shawnee not only as an economic threat but as a threat to their entire way of life.

9

CONCLUSION

ALTHOUGH THE SHAWNEE gave up any claim to land in
Kentucky in 1795, they had a profound influence on the early
history and the traditions and legends of the state. Unfortunately, much of the early record is marred by a hatred and
hostility between them and the settlers that led to the descrip-
tion of Kentucky as the "Dark and Bloody Ground." As land
speculators and settlers trickled and then swarmed over the
Appalachian Mountains, the Shawnee fought hard to retain
their hunting territory and homeland. The Shawnee also became a victim in the colonial land struggle between Pennsylvania and Virginia that resulted in Lord Dunmore's War.

These struggles became an important part of the history of
Kentucky's first settlements. The villages, including Harrodsburg and Boonesboro, had to be fortified against regular
attacks by the Indians. Shawnee hunting and raiding parties
attempted to drive the settlers back to Virginia by making hit-
and-run attacks on these early settlements. The result was that
a militia was sent to protect the settlers. Kentucky militiamen
pursued Shawnee raiding parties and often mounted counter-
raids on Shawnee villages as far north as the Little Miami
River in Ohio. The conflicts involved such men as George
Rogers Clark, Anthony Wayne, and William Henry Harrison.

The major adversaries of these military leaders were
Tecumseh and his brother Tenskwautawa, the Prophet. Te-

cumseh gathered a force from several tribes and made raids on the Kentucky settlements of Blue Licks on the Kentucky River and Bryan Station north of the present city of Lexington. Long after most other Shawnee made their peace with the Americans, Tecumseh continued his struggle until his death at the Battle of the Thames during the War of 1812. By this time he had been made a general in the British army.

Conflicts with the Shawnee have also become part of the history and legend of Daniel Boone. Separating fact from fiction regarding a man of Boone's stature is difficult. However, it is known that he was respected by the Shawnee for his tenacity. Both Boone and his daughter were captured by the Indians. His daughter was immediately recovered, but his own captivity saw him taken to Ohio where he was adopted by the Shawnee. Tales of his surviving the gauntlet have become a part of Boone's legend.

Other legends and stories of Shawnee captivity are a part of Kentucky's early history. These stories contain tales of depredations and heroics that inevitably spring from the struggles any people make to conquer and settle an area. Probably the best known is the story of Jenny Wiley, who survived several months of Shawnee captivity even after the Shawnee had killed her children. How much truth there is to these legends is irrelevant; they reflect the hatred and fear that the early settlers felt toward the Shawnee.

Another legend from eastern Kentucky is less negative in character. From 1760 to 1770 a man named Jonathan Swift is supposed to have worked some silver mines in the vicinity of Mud Lick Creek in Johnson County. The exact location is not known and many unsuccessful attempts have been made to find them. A part of this legend includes the use of Shawnee laborers. The story persists, not only in the hills of eastern Kentucky, but among the Shawnee as well. As late as 1870 a Shawnee from Oklahoma, a descendant of Chief Cornstalk, returned to the area in search of the mines.

Besides legends there were other things the Shawnee left behind that have become important parts of Kentucky's history. The Shawnee reputation in medicine was picked up by the early settlers who had left their doctors in the East. Snakeroot, willow bark, sassafras root, and ginseng root were among the numerous substances whose medicinal qualities were well known to Shawnee doctors. The early settlers learned how to prepare and use the plants from the Shawnee, and many Kentuckians still rely on these native medicines to cure common ailments.

Attention was drawn to the salt resources of the Ohio Valley by the Shawnee who manufactured and traded the commodity. With the curtailment of foreign imports the settlers learned from the Shawnee the location of valuable salt licks. Although other mineral resources eventually became much more important on the Allegheny frontier, salt was the first major industrial enterprise.

Shawnee trails crisscrossed the state of Kentucky and facilitated the settlement of the region. The most important was the Great Warriors Path which led through the Cumberland Gap, opening Kentucky to the Virginians. The Cumberland Trail connected the Ohio River to the Cumberland River at Nashville. In the western part of the state the Russellville-Shawneetown Trail led to Illinois. The early settlements of Harrodsburg and Boonesboro were situated on these Indian trails.

General Anthony Wayne's victory over the Shawnee at the battle of Fallen Timbers in 1794 virtually ended Shawnee influence in Kentucky. The subsequent Treaty of Greenville in 1795 forced the Shawnee to give up all claims to land south of the Ohio River. Many had given these up long before this, but this treaty closed to the Shawnee the only territory they could possibly consider as a homeland. A few remained on two reservations in northwestern Ohio, but in 1832 and 1833 they were forced to leave for a reservation in Kansas.

A new chapter was thus initiated in Shawnee history as they were pushed onto reservations and prohibited from pursuing their traditional nomadic way of life. By 1867 they were confined to three small reservations in Oklahoma with no control over their own destiny, living off meager annuity payments for land taken from them by fraud and force. For over one hundred years this once proud people has lived in virtual poverty, victim of the "manifest destiny" of a land-hungry civilization.

Bibliographical Essay

USEFUL MANUSCRIPT SOURCES for this book include state and national archives. The state archives of Pennsylvania and Ohio produced much regarding Shawnee settlements in these areas. One of the most valuable sources for material on Kentucky and the Ohio Valley was the Draper Papers of the Wisconsin Historical Society. On the national level the archives of the American Philosophical Society, the Library of Congress, and the National Archives were used.

Much of the relevant material was obtained from secondary sources and published documents. Of the latter the most useful in terms of land transactions and treaties included the *American State Papers* (Washington, D.C., 1832–1834) containing two volumes on Indian affairs; *Indian Affairs, Laws and Treaties* (Washington, D.C., 1904) edited by Charles Kappler; and Clarence Carter's edition of the *Territorial Papers of the United States* (Washington, D.C., 1934, 1937). Valuable information on Indian trade and trade relations was provided by *The Calendar of the Virginia State Papers* (Richmond, 1875) compiled by William P. Palmer; William McDowell's edited volume from the South Carolina archives of the *Journals of the Commissioners of the Indian Trade: September 20, 1710–August 29, 1718* (Columbia, 1955); and *The Papers of Sir William Johnson* (Albany, N.Y., 1921–1965). Besides these official papers and documents, original accounts of traders, missionaries, travelers, and explorers, edited and published by Reuben Gold Thwaites in two series, *Early Western Travels* (Cleveland, Ohio, 1904–1907) and *Jesuit Relations* (Cleveland, Ohio, 1896–1901), have been extensively consulted.

For ethnographic material, much use has been made of the

publications of Erminie Wheeler Voegelin. Her historical and ethnographic studies are the only modern works devoted specifically to the Shawnee. Her works include *Mortuary Customs of the Shawnee and Other Eastern Tribes* (Indianapolis, Ind., 1944), and several articles. Thomas Wildcat Alford, a Shawnee, has written two valuable works: "The Shawnee Indians," published in W. A. Galloway's *Old Chillicothe* (Xenia, Ohio, 1934), and *Civilization* (Norman, Okla., 1936). C. C. Trowbridge compiled the oral accounts of Black Hoof, a Shawnee chief, and Tenskwautawa, the Shawnee Prophet and brother of Tecumseh, in a volume entitled *Shawnese Traditions* (Ann Arbor, Mich., 1939) edited and published by Vernon Kinietz and Erminie W. Voegelin.

Other sources used in gathering ethnographic material on the Shawnee were: George P. Donehoo's "The Shawnee in Pennsylvania," *Western Pennsylvania Historical Magazine* 7 (1924):178–87; *Old Chillicothe* (Xenia, Ohio, 1934) by William A. Galloway; Sister Mary Henry O. P. Gibbs's "The Shawnee Indians" (M.A. thesis, Catholic University, 1932); *History of the Shawnee Indians* (Cincinnati, 1855) by Henry Harvey; "Shawnee" by James Mooney in F. W. Hodge's *Handbook of American Indians North of Mexico* (Washington, D.C., 1912); and Charles Callender's *Social Organization of the Central Algonkian Indians* (Milwaukee, Wis., 1962). Two articles by Joab Spencer useful for ethnographic material were: "The Shawnee Indians," *Transactions of the Kansas State Historical Society* 10 (1908):382–402, and "Shawnee Folk-Lore," *Journal of American Folk-Lore* 22 (1909):319–26. Bruno Nettl's article, "The Shawnee Musical Style," *Southwestern Journal of Anthropology* 9 (1953):277–85, provided much information about Shawnee cultural traits.

Useful secondary sources dealing with Shawnee-white interaction include: Thomas Abernathy's *Western Lands and the American Revolution* (New York, 1964); K. P. Bailey's edited volume of *The Ohio Company Papers, 1753–1817* (Ann Arbor, Mich., 1947); Charles A. Hanna's *The Wilderness Trail* (New York, 1911); Francis Parkman's *The Jesuits in North America* (Boston, 1867) and *Conspiracy of Pontiac* (Boston, 1878); Paul

C. Phillips's *The Fur Trade* (Norman, Okla., 1961); Francis Prucha's *American Indian Policy in the Formative Years* (Cambridge, Mass., 1962); and Joseph S. Walton's *Conrad Weiser and the Indian Policy of Pennsylvania* (Philadelphia, 1900).

Besides the Draper Papers there are other good sources dealing with the Shawnee in Kentucky. One of the best is Lucien Beckner's publication of "Eskippakithiki: The Last Indian Town in Kentucky," *Filson Club History Quarterly* 6 (1932):355–82. Willard Rouse Jillson has published two books with good information on the Shawnee: *The Big Sandy Valley; A Regional History prior to the Year 1850* (Louisville, Ky., 1923), and *Early Clark County, Kentucky, 1674–1824* (Frankfort, Ky., 1966). Biographies of Daniel Boone usually contain information on his relations with the Shawnee. Lyman Draper's unpublished "Life of Boone" is an excellent source.

Index

Abihka tribe, 21
Absentee Shawnee, 21, 25, 27
Alabama: Shawnee settlement of, 14-15, 20-21, 23, 58, 63, 67, 74-75; trade with Shawnee, 21, 75-76
American Revolution, 21, 85-87
Andaste tribe. *See* Conestoga tribe
Arkansas, Shawnee settlement of, 25
Arthur, Gabriel, 11

Black Hoof (Cathecassa), 14, 16, 29, 34, 41
Boone, Daniel, 2-3, 24, 87, 93
British: anti-French agitation of Shawnee, 73, 83; anti-U.S. agitation of Shawnee, 88-89; policy toward the Shawnee, 73, 76, 78-79, 86-89; and Shawnee land, 78-79, 82-84; Shawnee relations with the, 14, 23, 34, 73, 75-76, 78-79, 83-84, 86, 88-89, 91. *See also* specific colonies; trade
buffalo, 39-40, 45
Bullitt, Thomas, 3, 84
burial, 7-8, 50; cultural stability of, 50, 57; and name groups, 29, 50

Cahokia tribe, 14
Canada, original homeland in, 5. *See also* French

captives, 1, 16, 66, 93; adoption of white, 30, 93; black, 31; use of, 29, 31, 42. *See also* slaves
Catawba tribe, 18-20, 63, 65-67, 71
Central Algonquian, culture of, 28-29, 31-33, 57
ceremonies, 29, 32-33, 36, 38-39, 49, 52-53, 57; in the council house, 45; puberty, 29; seasonal agricultural, 29, 38, 49. *See also* medicine; religion
Chartier, Martin, 21, 74
Chartier, Peter, 15, 21, 66, 68, 74-75
Cherokee tribe, 9, 11, 14, 16, 18, 20-21, 27, 53, 56, 63, 65, 70
Chickasaw tribe, 14-15, 21, 63, 65-66, 71, 74
children, 29-30
Chillicothe division, 8-9, 16, 33, 85
Chippewa tribe, 87
Choctaw tribe, 52
clan system, 28-29, 32
Clark, George Rogers, 24, 92
clothing, 39, 42, 45-46, 52, 55, 57
Conestoga tribe, 19, 22, 63, 67-68
Congaree tribe, 18
Conoy tribe, 5
Cornstalk (Hokolesqua), 85-86
council house (msikamekwi), 45
councils, village, 36, 45

intermarriage, Shawnee-white, 74, 78

intertribal relations, 3, 59, 62-71. *See also* specific tribes

Iroquois tribe, 2, 9-12, 14-15, 20, 22-23, 33, 49, 58-59, 63, 67-71, 82, 84. *See also* trade

Jackson, Andrew, 25, 67

Jefferson, Thomas, 25

Johnston, John, 89

Joliet, Louis, 7, 13

Jones, David, 49, 56

Kakowatchekey, 56

Kansas, Shawnee settlement of, 25, 27, 41, 94

Kenton, Simon, 24

Kentucky: relations with the Shawnee, 1-3, 15-16, 18, 24, 34, 41, 83, 86-88, 92-94; Shawnee hunting in, 31; Shawnee industry in, 41, 93; Shawnee settlement of, 1-2, 6-7, 10-16, 18, 21, 23, 45, 63, 65, 74-75; white settlement of, 1-3, 84-85, 86-87, 92-94

Kickapoo tribe, 29, 34, 53, 70

kinship, with other tribes, 5-6, 53

Kispogogi division, 8, 13, 33

Knox, Henry, 87-88

land: fraudulent purchase of Shawnee, 79; impact of Shawnee loss of, on their economy, 3, 41-42, 90, 94-95; influence of negotiations for, on Shawnee-white relations, 73, 84, 88-90; influence of occupation of, on Shawnee-white relations, 1-3, 24, 56, 59, 73, 78-80, 82-92; negotiations for, with other tribes, 31, 59, 63, 82, 84; Shawnee, and

the French, 75-76, 78, 83; speculators' ploys to lure whites to, 2-3. *See also* treaties

language, 3, 5, 57-58

LaSalle, Sieur de, 7, 11-13, 74-75

law, 36-37, 49

Lord Dunmore's War, 84-85, 92

Loup nation, 13

Louisiana Purchase, Shawnee settlement of, 25, 90

Marquette, Jacques, 7, 12-13

marriage, 29-30

Marston, Morrell, 6

Maryland, Shawnee settlement of, 12, 19

Mascoutin tribe, 11

Massachusetts, relations with the Shawnee, 10

material culture, 8, 55, 80. *See also* specific crafts and technologies

medicine, 33, 48-50, 93-94

Mequachake division, 8, 13, 33, 53

mercenaries, use of Shawnee as, 62-63

Miami tribe, 5, 8, 11-12, 29, 34, 36, 59, 63, 69-70, 87

migration, 3-6, 31, 41, 43, 59-63

military alliances, Shawnee-white, 73. *See also* specific colonies, countries, tribes

Mingo tribe, 23, 69, 87

mining, white use of Shawnee in, 1, 16, 18, 93

Minquas tribe. *See* Conestoga tribe

Miseekwaaweekwaakee, legend of, 29

missionaries, 48-49, 56. *See also* John Heckewelder; David Jones; Moravians; Quakers; religion

Treaty of Camp Charlotte, 85-86
Treaty of Greenville, 16, 24, 34, 88, 94
Treaty of Lancaster, 82
tribal chief, 33
tribal divisions, 8-10, 32-33, 53. *See also* Chillicothe; Hathawekela; Kispogogi; Mequachake; Piqua

U.S.: government: annuity payments, 34, 90, 95; Indian policy, 25, 86-87, 89-90; legislation concerning Shawnee, 86-88; and Shawnee migration, 25, 27, 59; warfare with Shawnee, 34, 87-88, 90-91

Vandalia scheme, 84
Vielle, Arant, 22
village: as an economic unit, 29, 31, 38; as an organizational unit, 28, 30-33, 57, 67; as a ritual unit, 28-29, 49; split during hunting season, 2, 31, 38-39, 57
village chief, 29, 33-34, 36
Virginia: policy toward Shawnee, 78; relations with Shawnee, 65, 82-86, 92; settlement of Shawnee land by, 2, 82, 84-85, 94; Shawnee settle-

ment of, 9, 19, 23; trade with the Shawnee, 16

war chief, 33-34, 36
War of 1812, 70, 88; Shawnee participation in, 25, 34, 52, 70, 89, 93
warfare: intertribal, 62-63, 65-68, 70; Shawnee-white, 52, 70, 73, 78, 84-88, 90-91. *See also* specific wars, colonies, countries
Washington, George, 2, 84
Wayne, Anthony, 24, 88, 92, 94
weapons, 55, 58, 80
Weiser, Conrad, 69, 81
West Virginia, Shawnee settlement of, 19
Western Confederacy, 69. *See also* Miami, Delaware, and Wyandot tribes
Westo tribe, 18, 63-66
Wichita tribe, 63
wigwam (wegiwa), 43-45
Wiley, Jenny, 16, 93
Winnebago tribe, 6
witchcraft, 48-50
Wyandot tribe, 34, 63, 69-70, 87

Yamasee War, 20-21, 80
Yuchi tribe, 13, 20